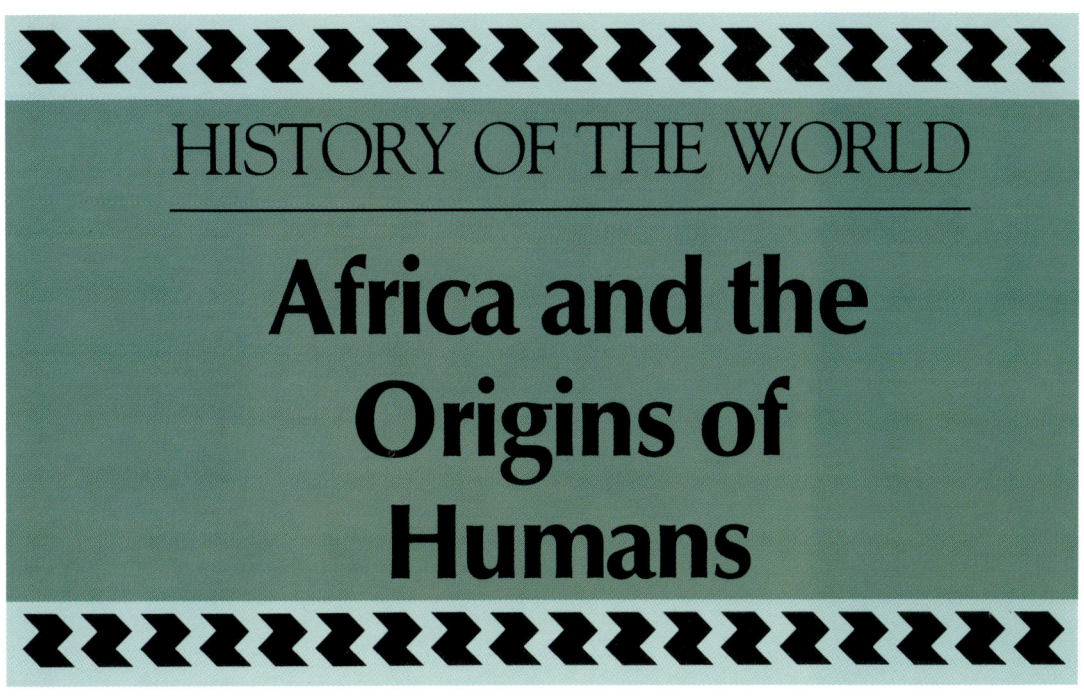

CHERRYTREE BOOKS

A Cherrytree Book

This edition adapted by
A S Publishing

First published by Editoriale Jaca Book s.p.a. Milan
© Editoriale Jaca 1987
First English edition published in United States
by Raintree Publishers
English translation © Raintree Publishers Limited Partnership
Translation by Hess-Inglin Translation Service

This edition first published 1990
by Cherrytree Press Ltd
a subsidiary of
The Chivers Company Ltd
Windsor Bridge Road
Bath, Avon BA2 3AX

Copyright © Cherrytree Press Ltd 1990

British Library Cataloguing in Publication Data
Africa and the origins of humans.
  I. Williams, Brian II. Series III. Origini dell'uomo e
l'Africa. *English*
573.2

ISBN 0-7451-5103-5

Printed in Hong Kong by Imago Publishing Ltd

All rights reserved. No part of this publication may be reproduced, stored in a retrieval system, or transmitted, in any form or by any means without the prior permission in writing of the publisher, nor be otherwise circulated in any form of binding or cover other than that in which it is published and without a similar condition including this condition being imposed on the subsequent publisher

Contents

Unity and Diversity in Africa	6
The Search for Human Origins	8
Monkeys and Hominids	10
From Hominids to Humans: *Homo habilis*	12
The First Conquest of the World	14
Homo sapiens	16
The Birth of Culture	18
Adaptations to the Sahara	20
The Discovery of the Great Forest	22
The Expansion into Southern Africa	24
The Tribes of the North	26
People of the Waters	28
The Blossoming of the Desert	30
The Birth of Egyptian Society	32
Everyday Life in Egypt	34
The Middle and New Kingdoms	36
The Egyptian Religion	38
Humanity's Place in the Universe	40
Shepherds, Blacksmiths, and Merchants	42
Carthage: Its Birth and Development	44
Carthage: Art and Trade	46
The Kingdom of Kush	48
Meroe, Capital of the Kush Kingdom	50
The Kingdom of Aksum	52
Aksum: Trade, Religion, Culture	54
The Greek Colonies in Libya and Egypt	56
The Greeks Conquer Ègypt	58
Egypt During the Hellenistic Period	60
The Romans Conquer Africa	62
Egypt Under Rome	64
Roman Africa	66
Christianity	68
Glossary	73
Index	77

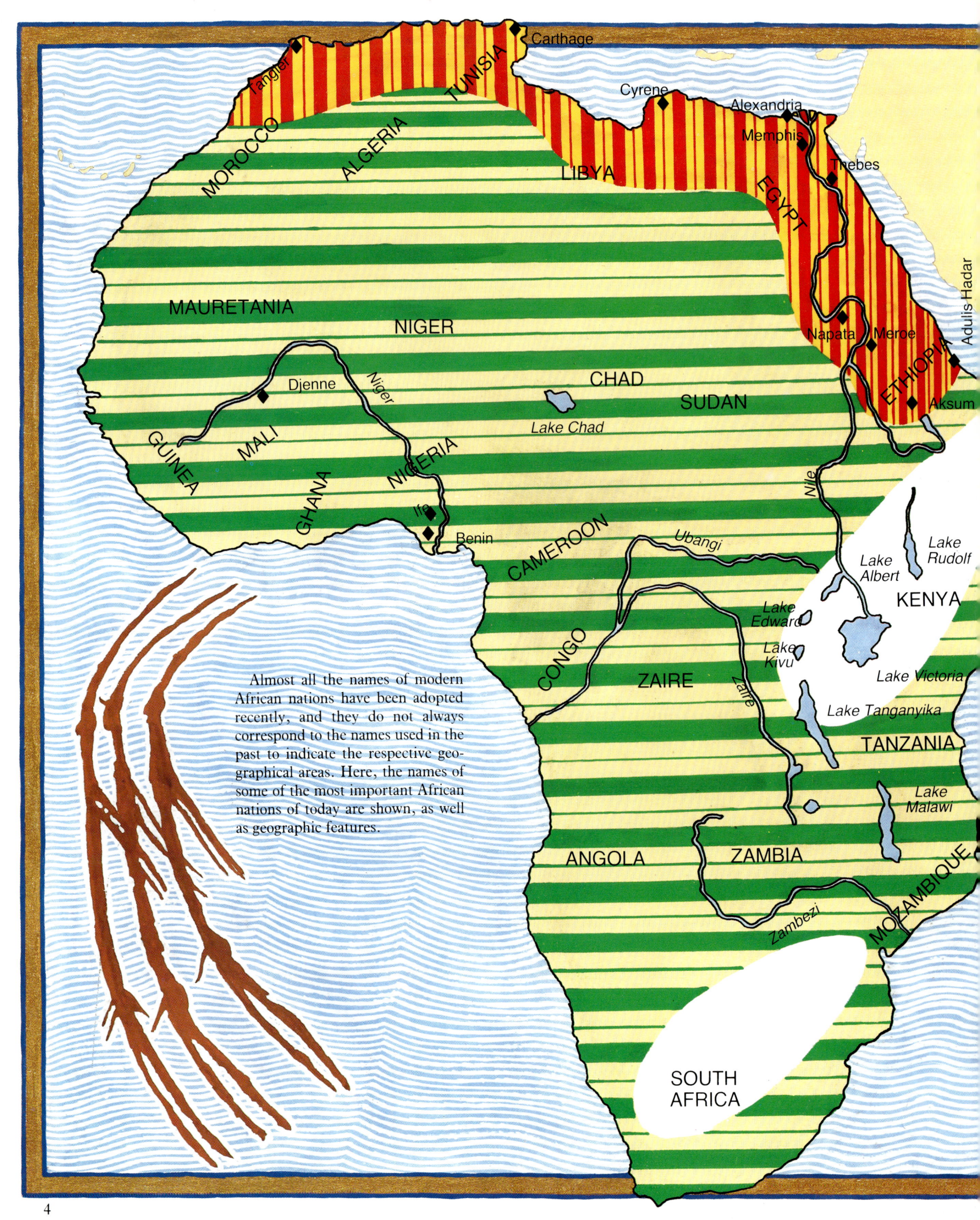

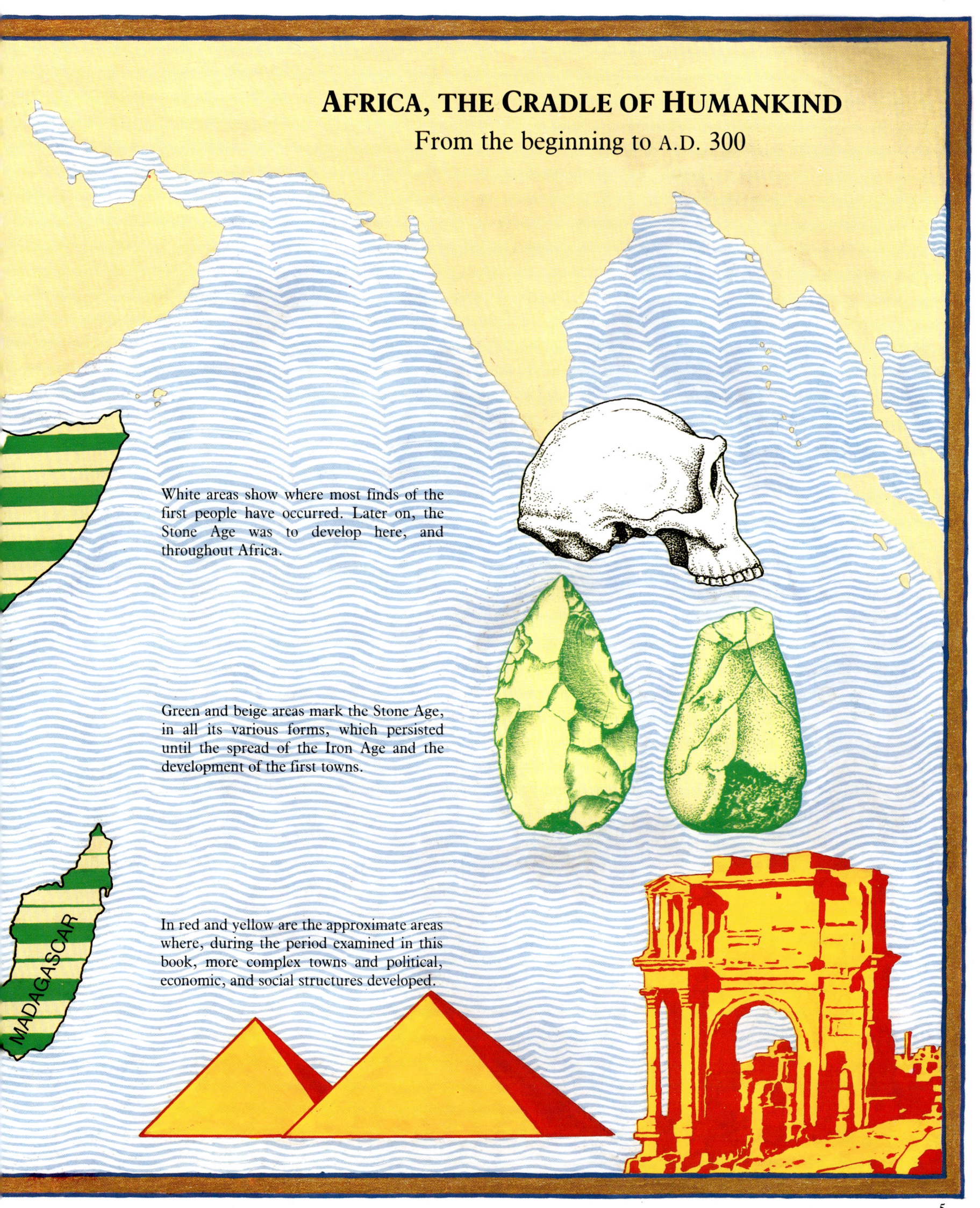

UNITY AND DIVERSITY IN AFRICA

Many anthropologists have called Africa the cradle of humankind. This is because scientists have found many fossils of ape-like and human-like creatures which lived in East Africa over the last 4 million years. From these fossils, scientists are trying to discover how the human race evolved.

Africa is a landmass with a relatively straight coastline. Its vast expanse of 30 million square kilometres is centred on the equator but stretches far into both hemispheres. Within this great continent, various habitats are clearly defined. These habitats develop in certain areas, called belts, which extend both north and south from the equator. Most of Africa is an exceptionally old and stable landmass, but there are regions where change is happening. A region's stability depends on the age of its rock formations. Ancient formations have slowly settled over millions of years, while erosion has smoothed and simplified the landscape.

In the eastern part of the continent, however, the earth's crust is still splitting and being pulled apart. Mountains are still being lifted, and volcanoes fill valleys with lava. The area of greatest activity is called the Great Rift Valley, a zigzag-shaped split 3,000 kilometres (km) long. Some mountains in this area are over 5,000 metres (m) high, while two-thirds of the African landmass is covered by plateaus (flat tablelands) nearly 1,000 m high.

A Continental Climate of Extremes

Much of Africa is a high plateau surrounded by steep slopes that lead down to narrow coastal plains. The cool uplands have proved more attractive to human settlement than the humid, unhealthy coastal plains. The uplands were the centres of most early black African civilizations and also of the recent colonial empires. As a result, coastal transport and communications never fully developed, except along the east coast and in the Mediterranean and Red seas. Rivers were important lines of communications, though often interrupted by waterfalls.

While the high plateaus and mountains of Africa have a moderate climate, other areas have more extreme continental climates. The Sahara desert has high temperatures throughout the year, but enormous changes in temperature often occur on a daily basis, with extremely hot days and very cold nights.

Africa has the world's biggest desert, but also abundant inland water. It boasts the world's longest river, the Nile, and a chain of lakes whose total water volume and surface area are rarely equalled. The variations in these basins, both yearly and over the centuries, have also affected human history on the continent, especially in areas where green and life-laden habitats periodically turn into deserts.

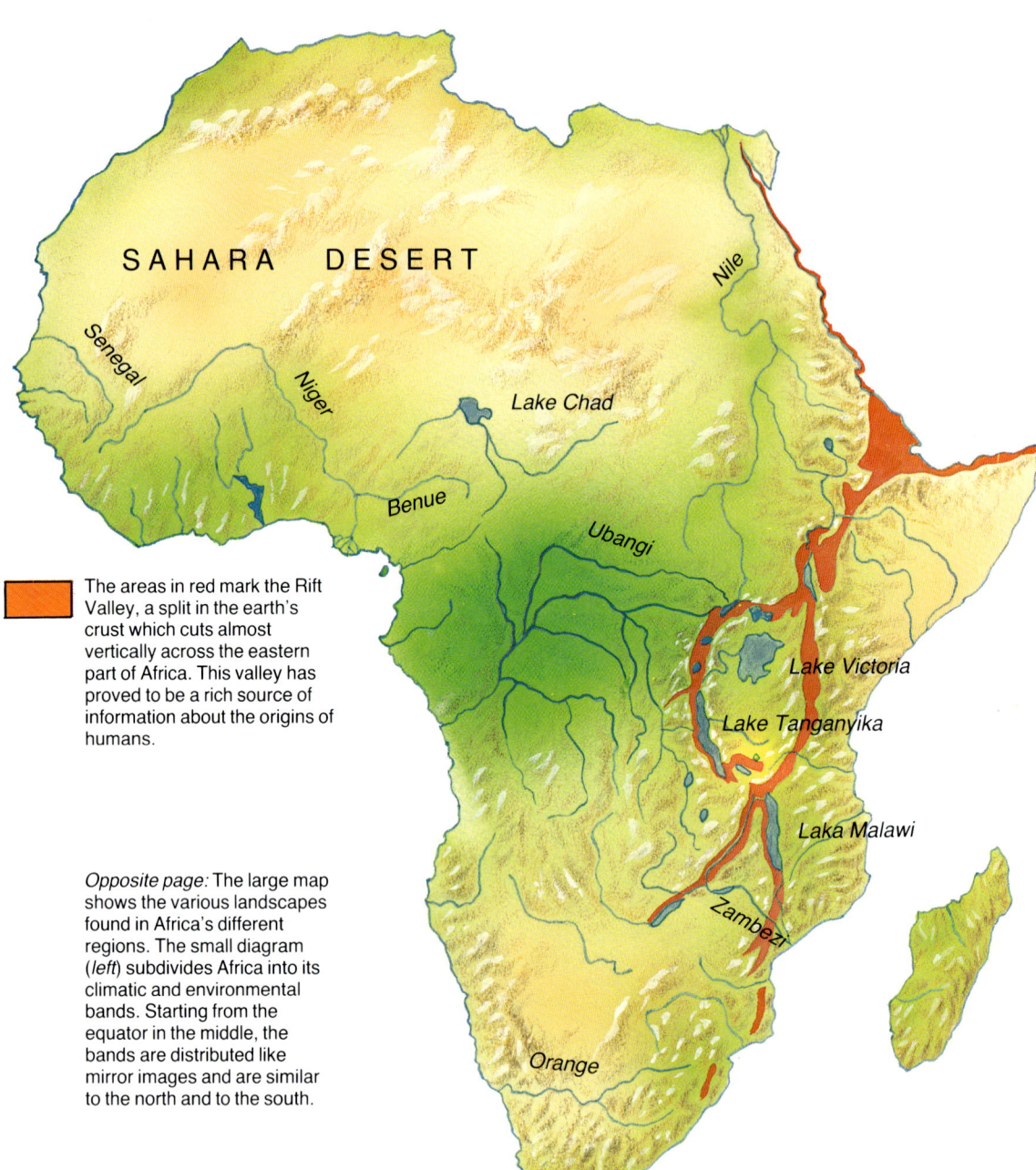

The areas in red mark the Rift Valley, a split in the earth's crust which cuts almost vertically across the eastern part of Africa. This valley has proved to be a rich source of information about the origins of humans.

Opposite page: The large map shows the various landscapes found in Africa's different regions. The small diagram (*left*) subdivides Africa into its climatic and environmental bands. Starting from the equator in the middle, the bands are distributed like mirror images and are similar to the north and to the south.

A Slice of the Globe

Africa covers a vast slice of the globe running from north to south and hosts a wide range of environments and climates. The continent's climate and vegetation develop in belts around the equator. In the centre, or heart, of the continent is the equatorial rain forest, along which the Zaire (Congo) River branches out. Around this belt, to the north and to the south, stretch the rings of savannas.

Lush savanna merges into the semi-arid Sahel, which has grassy vegetation. Adjoining the Sahel are semi-desert and desert, parts of which are mountainous. Further to the north is the largest desert in the world, the Sahara, a name which means "absolute emptiness." At the top is the scrub zone. In the northern desert the vegetation is of the Mediterranean scrub type, while in the southern hemisphere this scrub is called fynbos.

An exceptionally varied world of animal life has developed in these different areas. The abundance of large animals was useful to humans, who hunted wild game for food and raw materials. On the other hand, many small animals such as insects have proved harmful to humankind. Along the coastal plains or near inland water, for example, human populations have been thinned or driven away by malaria, schistosomiasis, and sleeping sickness.

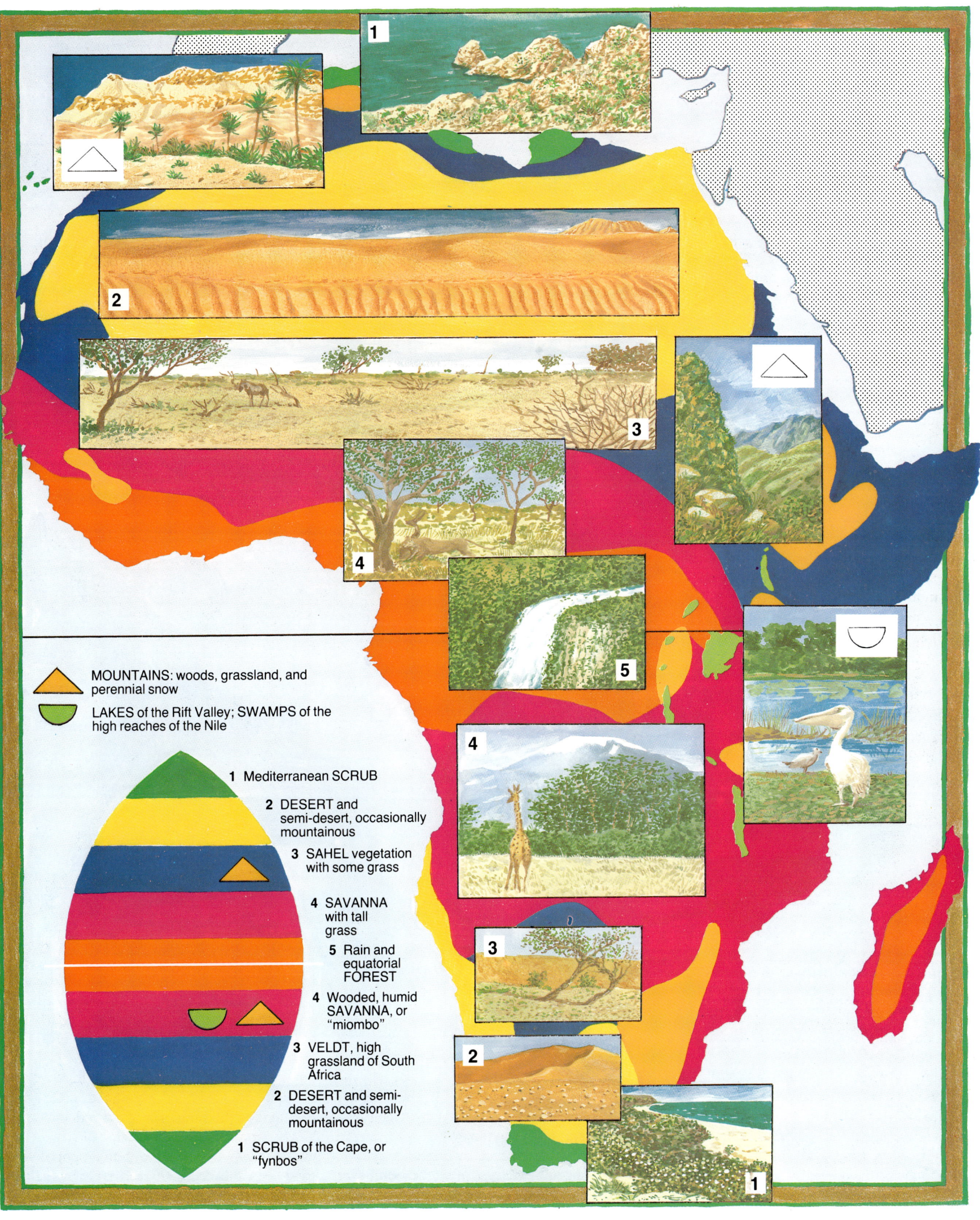

The Search for Human Origins

Since the nineteenth century, there has been a growing interest in the search for human origins in every part of the world. In the last century, scientists discovered how people are linked to the rest of nature, and that a chain of living beings connects all humans to similar species of the past. This is called evolution.

Human history developed within the history of a larger group of beings—that of the apes, or Primates. This development took place over millions of years and the history of its progress is learned through fossils, which are very ancient skeletal remains that document the physical evolution of human ancestors, as well as that of other, now extinct, species. Africa offers much evidence—both animal and environmental—which reveals the story of the rise of humankind.

Fossilized History

Fossil remains of apes and humans are sparse. To be preserved, bones and teeth must escape decay. The body of a dead animal on the forest floor has no chance of escaping decay. To be preserved, it must be rapidly buried in the muddy bottom of a river or of a quiet pond. The body of a savanna primate would leave even fewer traces. The best chance for its preservation would be for a large animal to carry it into a cave or abandon it under a shower of volcanic ash. The first humanlike creatures, or hominids, inhabited the savanna. Their remains were sometimes preserved.

But how do researchers go about studying the origins of humans? Searching for fossils is a basic method. This calls for wide-range exploration of territories where rocks may contain good specimens. Fossils, objects, and tracks are all good sources of information, and the information is usually preserved under the ground. Excavations are an important scientific method of studying fossils from which scientists can determine their order and their relationship within the varying layers of soil. Further information can be gained from the remains by comparing their features with other fossils and living animals or plants.

A New Idea in Human History

In 1871, the British naturalist Charles Darwin first suggested that the "cradle" of humankind was to be found in warm areas and attracted attention to Africa. Darwin could not prove his idea, as human fossils had not been found when he first published his theory on the gradual transformation of species. Still, his idea was proved correct by researchers who began to look for traces of the ancestors of humankind. After half a century, the fossil hunt had turned into serious research.

The first remote human ancestor, however, was discovered very far away from Africa. In 1891 a Dutch doctor, Eugène Dubois, found traces of a prehistoric human being on the

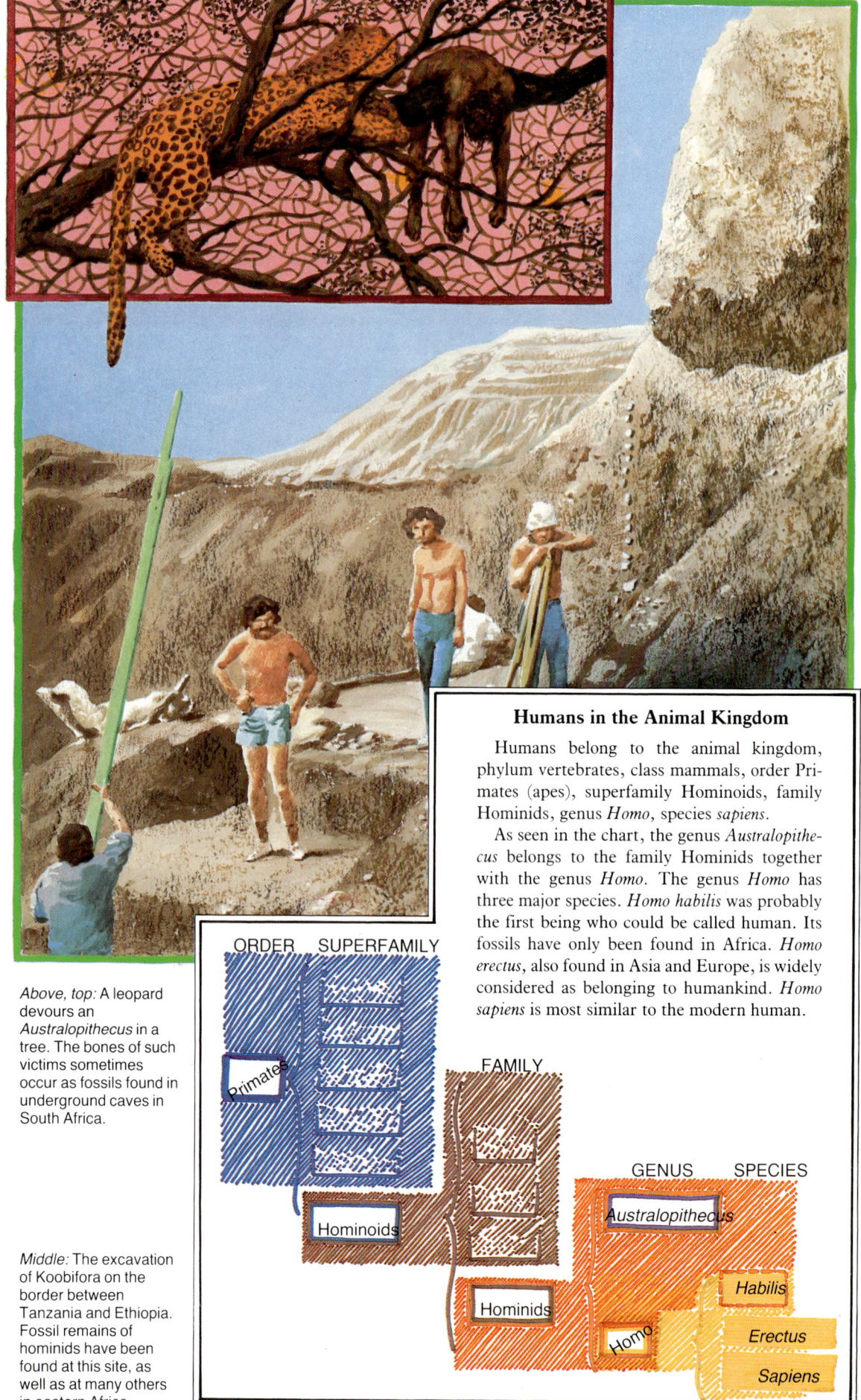

Above, top: A leopard devours an *Australopithecus* in a tree. The bones of such victims sometimes occur as fossils found in underground caves in South Africa.

Middle: The excavation of Koobifora on the border between Tanzania and Ethiopia. Fossil remains of hominids have been found at this site, as well as at many others in eastern Africa.

Humans in the Animal Kingdom

Humans belong to the animal kingdom, phylum vertebrates, class mammals, order Primates (apes), superfamily Hominoids, family Hominids, genus *Homo*, species *sapiens*.

As seen in the chart, the genus *Australopithecus* belongs to the family Hominids together with the genus *Homo*. The genus *Homo* has three major species. *Homo habilis* was probably the first being who could be called human. Its fossils have only been found in Africa. *Homo erectus*, also found in Asia and Europe, is widely considered as belonging to humankind. *Homo sapiens* is most similar to the modern human.

The Dutch doctor Eugène Dubois (1858-1940) found a series of fossil remains in Java, which he attributed to a species of hominid, called *Pithecanthropus*. The drawing shows a reconstruction of the skull of this species.

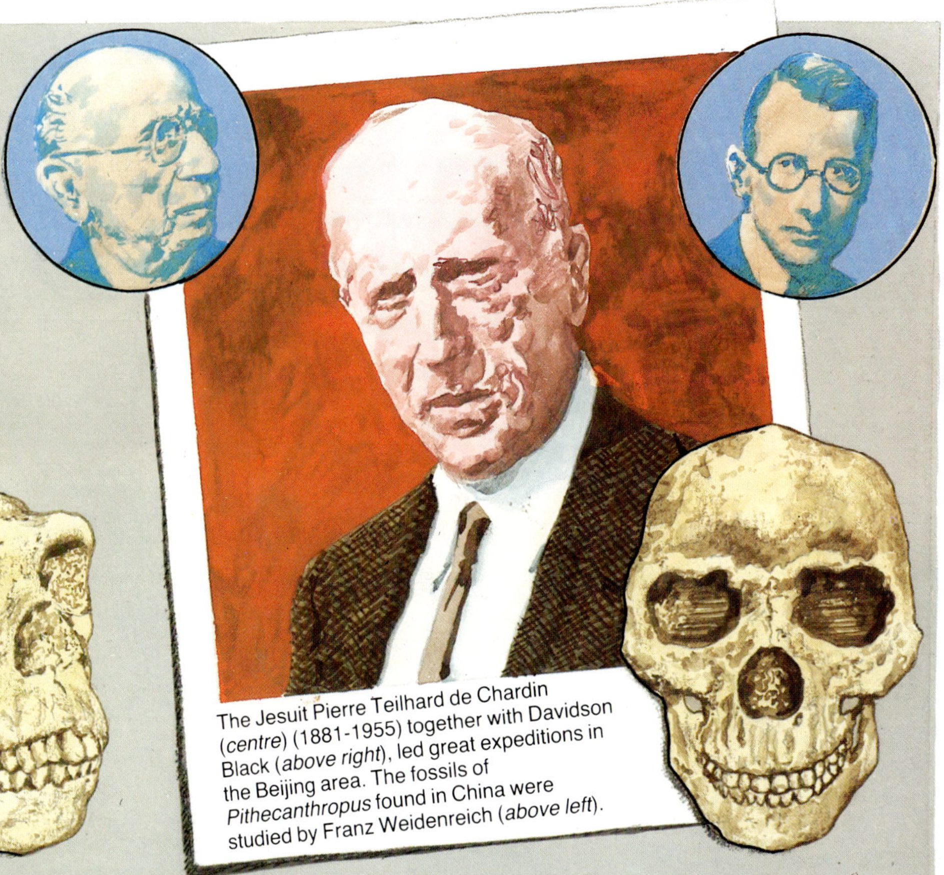

The Jesuit Pierre Teilhard de Chardin (*centre*) (1881-1955) together with Davidson Black (*above right*), led great expeditions in the Beijing area. The fossils of *Pithecanthropus* found in China were studied by Franz Weidenreich (*above left*).

Australopithecus remains were first discovered by Raymond Dart, an Australian anthropologist. Dart found a child's skull near Taung in southwest Africa. The creature, which was called *Australopithecus africanus*, had features between those of an ape and those of a human.

Louis Leakey (1903-1972) and his wife, Mary, discovered major sites with remains of hominids in Kenya and Tanzania. In 1959, they found the skull of an *Australopithecus*, which they called *Zinjanthropus boisei*.

island of Java, in Indonesia. It was a sensational discovery. For thirty years, Asia was considered the birthplace of humankind. This belief was strengthened by the discovery of similar fossil remains in China.

In the meantime, the search for human origins extended farther. In 1925, the Australian Raymond Dart found a skull in the Transvaal region of South Africa. It was older than the one which Dubois had found, similar to a chimpanzee's but with some human features. Dart called the specimen *Australopithecus*, which means "humanlike monkey of southern Africa." Although Dart's ideas were rejected by many, everyone's attention turned to Africa. In 1936 an inspired amateur, Robert Broom, discovered a series of important remains near Johannesburg in South Africa. These finds confirmed the identity of *Australopithecus*.

But Africa's real time of glory began in 1959 and is still going on today. The landmark event was the discovery, in eastern Africa, of an *Australopithecus* that turned out to be almost two million years old. This find crowned several years of determined exploration in Tanzania by anthropologists Louis and Mary Leakey. Since then, expeditions from many countries have travelled to the Rift valley. Through their work, four million years of human evolution are slowly coming to light.

baboon

gibbon

gorilla

chimpanzee

The similarity between humans and apes has always aroused curiosity. Even today, in the study of fossils, remains of apes are compared to those of humans to determine the main differences between the two groups.

This chart shows the relationships between the sequence of prehistoric periods and the species of hominids.

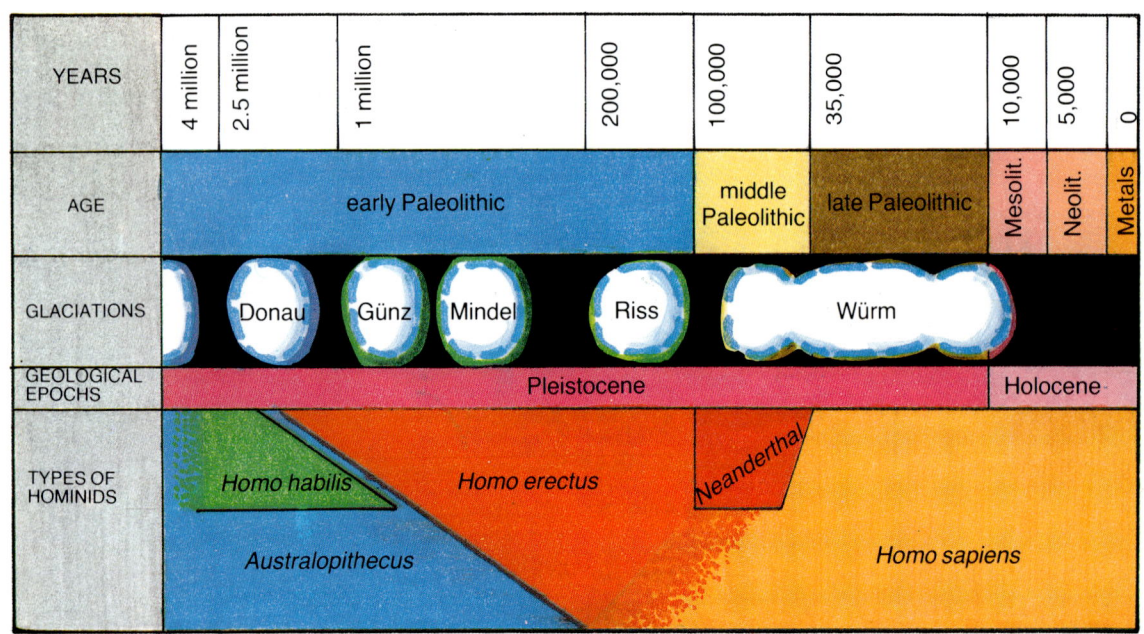

MONKEYS AND HOMINIDS

Long before early humans discovered the use of fire or learned to walk on two legs, their animal relatives had lived on the earth for at least sixty million years. Monkeys and apes had developed adaptations for a life spent in the trees of the tropical forest. They had four very mobile limbs, sensitive hands and feet, sharp three-dimensional vision, a weak sense of smell, a short snout, and a brain that was rapidly increasing in size and complexity. Many of these features were part of the biological traits passed on to humans.

"Lucy" and the Tracks of Laetoli

The first humanlike creatures, sometimes called pre-australopithecines, developed throughout Africa over four million years ago. They stood upright and walked on their hind legs, but their brains were smaller than those of today's humans (as the casts made from fossil skulls show). They had teeth that were closer to those of humans than of apes, and they had short front limbs which they used to climb trees when threatened.

Two remarkable discoveries have provided information on the pre-australopithecines. The first discovery took place in the Afar triangle (a wild region of northern Ethiopia). There, in 1974, an expedition led by American anthropologist Donald Johanson found over fifty-two bones of a humanlike skeleton. The great number of bones discovered allowed the researchers to reconstruct the creature. It proved to be a new species about three million years old, and was named *Australopithecus afarensis*. It came to be known as "Lucy," however, from the Beatles' song "Lucy in the Sky with Diamonds" to which the expedition members listened in the evenings at their campsite.

The second discovery took place in Laetoli, Tanzania. There in 1978, Mary Leakey discovered impressive evidence of the existence of a two-footed, sociable species of hominid that lived in the Pliocene epoch. Over 3,750,000 years ago, various animals left their tracks on a stretch of savanna where the soil was regularly covered by ashes from a nearby volcano. The soil on which the tracks were left was rapidly buried, thus preserving impressions in it. Tracks of elephants, birds, and beetles were preserved, together with those of beings whose feet and gait resembled humans. The study of these tracks suggests that they were left by two adults and a child, perhaps a family.

Eventually, the remains of over seventy

individuals belonging to this hominid group were collected. The shape of the thighbone and the position of the skull of these beings are proof that such creatures walked on two feet at least four million years ago. Remains also show that these early humans had highly mobile joints and could certainly climb trees. Males of the species were larger than the females, but all stood about 1 to 1.5 metres tall. Their front limbs were long and their hands were highly prehensile (adapted for grasping). Members of this species also had small heads, but their brains were partitioned similarly to the modern human brain.

This scene from the life of the early australopithecines was reconstructed from a path of tracks left on volcanic terrain in Laetoli, Tanzania, three million years ago.

The map charts the main sites where remains of hominids have been found.

Right: The footprints at Laetoli, which were found by Mary Leakey. *Far right:* The skeleton of an adult female, called Lucy, was found in Hadar, Ethiopia. It is the oldest, most complete fossil specimen of a hominid in existence.

Above: A nomadic group of australopithecines stops to rest.
Left: Reconstruction showing the appearance and face of *Zinjanthropus boisei*.

FROM HOMINIDS TO HUMANS: *HOMO HABILIS*

From the finds of the Afar region, it is obvious that the hominids had begun to multiply. Very quickly, they would start to branch out. In the illustration above a group of australopithecines is pictured; on the page opposite is a new species of the genus *Homo*, called *Homo habilis*. Many scholars consider these to be the first real humans.

The Evolution of *Australopithecus*

In 1924 a geologist from Johannesburg, Professor R.B. Joung, found a small skull in the office of a mine manager. He took the fossil to his friend Raymond Dart, an expert in anatomy. In 1925, Dart proclaimed the skull to be a new primate, which he named *Australopithecus africanus*. Dart was right. Although everyone expected to find that human ancestors were apes with large heads, even the pre-australopithecines had small heads and bodies (as described earlier). Yet they were obviously part of the evolutionary line.

Australopithecus africanus was the oldest and most frail of all true *Australopithecus* species. After Lucy and the tracks of Laetoli, other remains were found both in southern and eastern Africa. These remains from *Australopithecus africanus* proved to be between two million and three million years old. This human was about 1.25 m tall and weighed 25 to 30 kilograms (kg). The creature's face had prominent features, especially around the jaws. Its teeth were strong and well-suited for a vegetarian diet (although small animals were occasionally eaten).

Almost at the same time, *Australopithecus robustus* and *Zinjanthropus boisei* developed in southern and eastern Africa respectively. They appeared about two million years ago. These hominids were about 1.5 m tall and weighed 50 kg. Their diet consisted mainly of tough foods such as roots and tubers. Their extremely strong teeth became increasingly even, and their faces were more flattened than those of either *Australopithecus africanus* or the pre-australopithecines. All three species coexisted for a period of time.

The group life of the *Australopithecus* was organized to some degree, and they would gather at least temporarily in dwelling areas. From what has been found, the australopithecines seem to have been the first hominids able to manufacture tools. They were no longer merely felling a tree to cross a stream, or using a branch or a bone to strike something. They were actually making their own tools. The oldest known deposit of chipped stones was found in Omo, Ethiopia. The stones were discovered between layers of sedimentary rock that ranged from one million to four million years old.

Homo Habilis

The fossil remains of hominids with features more modern than the *Australopithecus* were found in east Africa. In 1964, Louis Leakey, Philip Tobias, and John Napier named this genus of hominid *Homo*. The first species of this genus was called *Homo habilis*. This species stemmed from the *Australopithecus*, but for a period the two coexisted. The oldest known fossil of *Homo habilis* is about two million years old.

Homo habilis is not considered a represent-

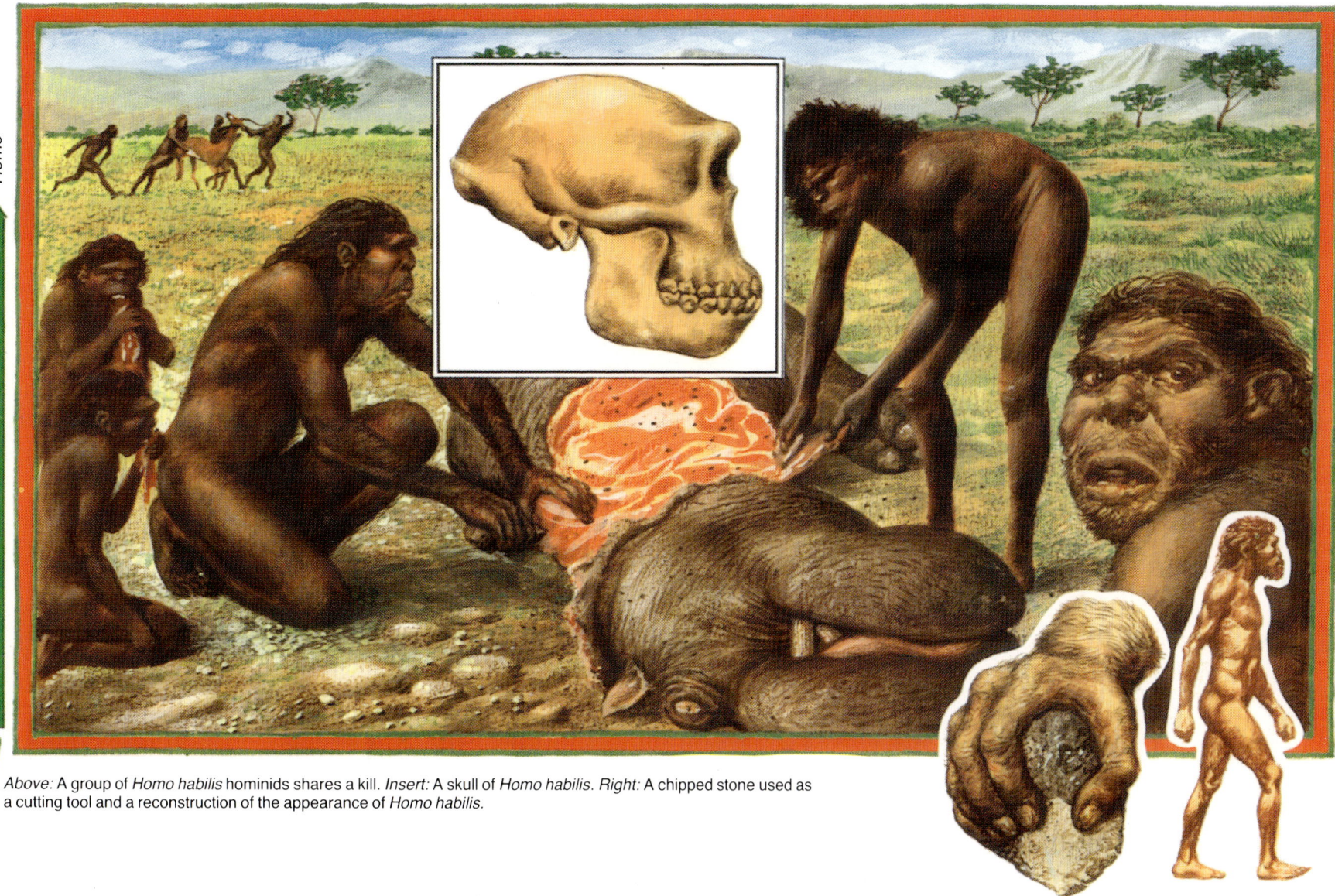

Above: A group of *Homo habilis* hominids shares a kill. *Insert:* A skull of *Homo habilis*. *Right:* A chipped stone used as a cutting tool and a reconstruction of the appearance of *Homo habilis*.

ative of humankind simply because of the ability to make tools. In fact, the australopithecines, which were certainly not yet human beings, also had such skills. *Homo habilis*, however, began to cut stones and bones in large quantities, as the finds collected at Olduvai in Tanzania show. These humans not only chipped stones, but they also used large stones to make various tools.

The Human

Unlike the ancestors of today's large apes that remained in the forests, *Homo habilis* began to venture out into the savanna. There, humans would eventually develop. But away from the forest, these hominids were unprotected. Neither did they have the strength of their relatives of the *Australopithecus robustus* species. The two species shared the same territory for a long time but probably did not interfere with each other. It might seem that *Homo habilis* was doomed to failure. But what these humans lacked in size and strength, they made up for in determination and intellect. Their success signalled a new course of evolution. The ability of these new beings to defend themselves and to survive was due to new features that they did not share with their ancestors.

In passing from pre-australopithecines to *Australopithecus*, and from *Australopithecus* to *Homo*, the skull was greatly changed. Such outward changes were proof of changes taking place in the brain. Of course, scientists cannot study the actual brains of these early humans. What they know of changes in the brain comes from studying fossilized skulls. By studying the internal shape of the skull, scientists can learn about the shape and the subdivisions of the brain itself. From such studies, it is known that the brain of *Homo habilis* was similar to that of the modern human. The brain of the later *Homo erectus* was even more developed. But it was not until *Homo sapiens*, the species to which people today belong, that the brain reached its present size.

The Question of Human Origin

At different times, three ideas have been proposed to explain the origin of humans:

(1) Humans are the inevitable result of evolution, which began from the original association of amino acids in the earth's early existence.

(2) Humans are a chance outcome of evolution.

(3) Humans first appeared on this earth the way they are today.

For a long time, these three ideas opposed each other. None of them alone seems to explain all the evidence available as yet. Evolution and the history of life seem to have worked together toward the development of humans. Thus, people did not appear ready-made on earth (3), did not originate by chance (2), and were not the inevitable outcome of an evolution involving a primeval "soup" of amino acids (1).

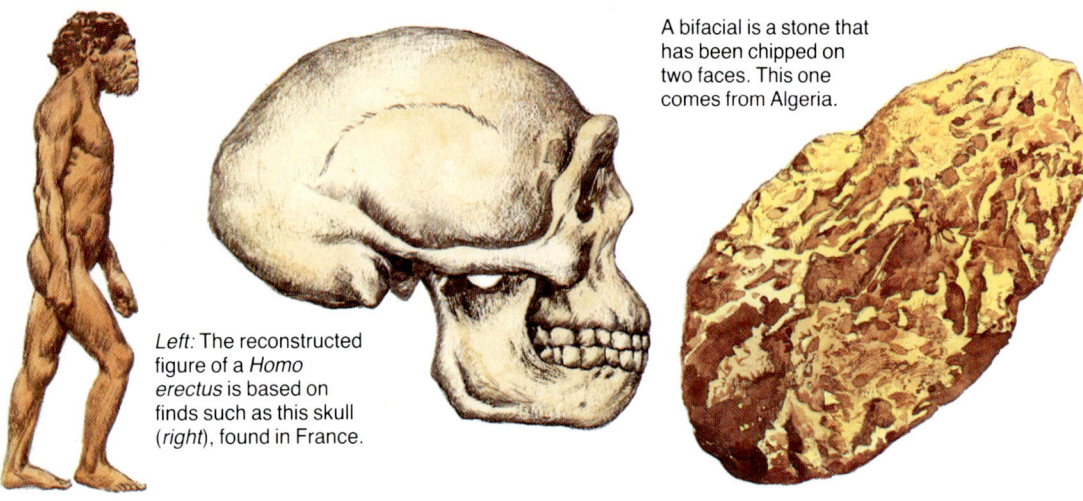

A bifacial is a stone that has been chipped on two faces. This one comes from Algeria.

Left: The reconstructed figure of a *Homo erectus* is based on finds such as this skull (*right*), found in France.

THE FIRST CONQUEST OF THE WORLD

Gradually, hominids spread throughout the world, reaching the regions around the Mediterranean Sea and Asia. This was a slow conquest of varied environments by a species whose population was still small. Around a million and a half years ago, a new subspecies of human developed in eastern Africa. Traces of similar individuals have been found from China to southern Europe. The first traces of fire, found in a site in the Kenyan Rift Valley, date back to the same period. This new kind of human was called *Homo erectus*.

Homo Erectus

Several human characteristics developed in the species *Homo erectus:* gait, hand skills, social structure, and language. The size and complexity of the brain also increased greatly. All members of this species, in spite of variations from place to place, had large, square faces. Their large eye sockets were framed by jutting forehead bones, and their mouths were enlarged by bulky teeth.

Most likely, facial expressions had developed within earlier groups where smiles, eye movements, and facial wrinkles were used to communicate. But by the time of *Homo erectus* spoken language was probably widespread. The study of skulls (and thus, indirectly, the brain) provides this information. As discussed earlier, scientists learn about brain development by studying the skull's inner shape. It has been found that in *Homo erectus*, the section of the brain that controlled language and the use of sound was well developed. Undoubtedly, *Homo erectus* did a great deal of communicating through sounds.

By the Fire

Few sites have provided skeletal remains of *Homo erectus* (see map opposite). Deposits of

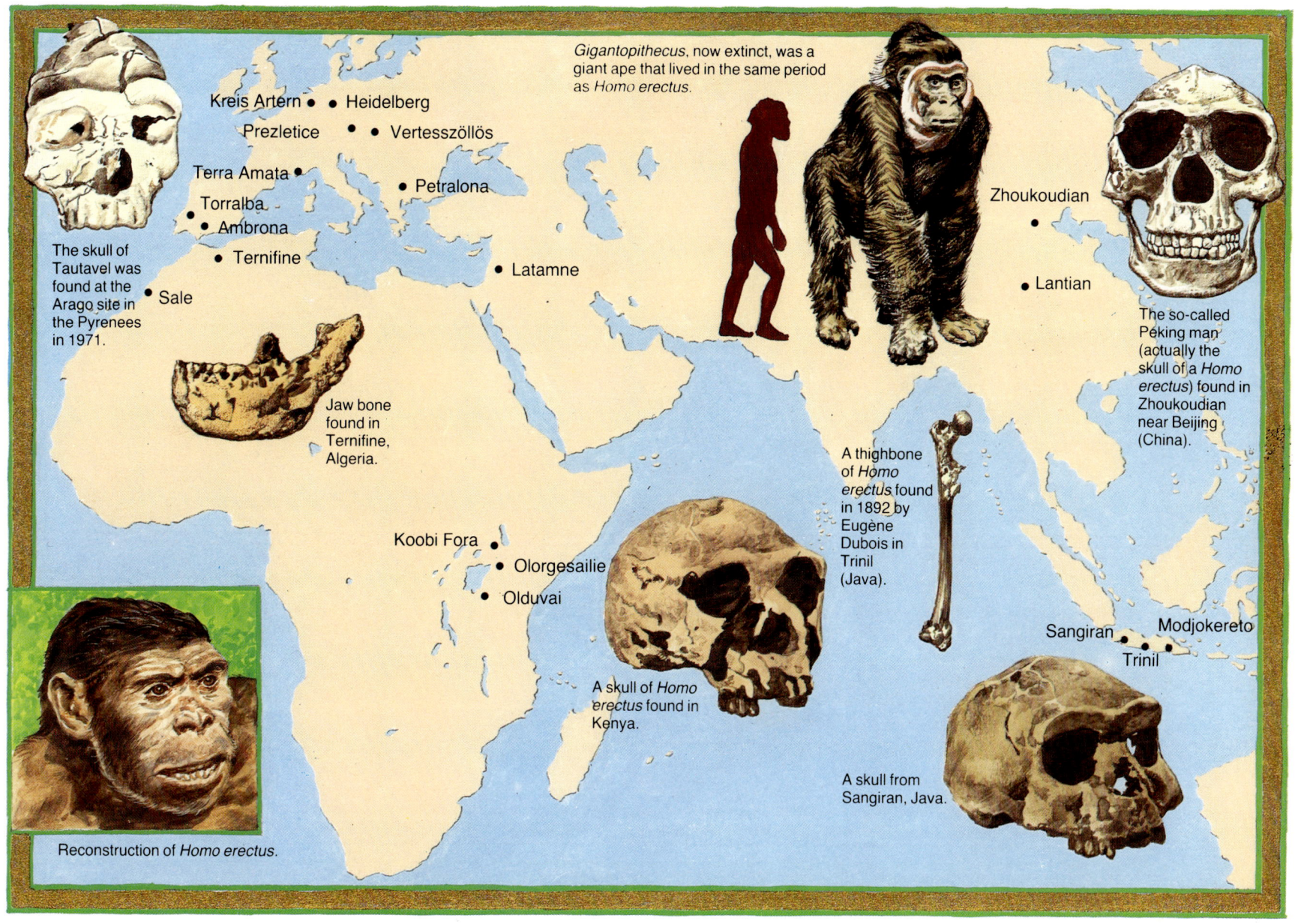

Opposite page, top: In this night scene, individuals of the genus *Homo* are gathered by a fire. Fire was a major discovery.

This map shows how widespread *Homo erectus* was. Skeletal finds show that this early human's distribution covered Africa, Asia, and Europe with varying populations.

chipped stones—signs of camps made by these people—are found more frequently. Such sites sometimes also contained other evidence of the daily lives of these human ancestors. From these finds, scientists were able to reconstruct nocturnal fire circles, where daily experiences, as well as meat from hunted game, were shared. In this way, the process of chipping a stone until it had a sharp, easy-to-hold shape was also traced.

Homo erectus gradually settled in all the temperate and tropical territories, spreading throughout Africa, Asia, and Europe. It is not known for sure when humans entered Europe. But they gradually adapted to the European environments of the Atlantic coasts and the central-northern regions. Settlements in these areas are proof of human adaptability to an environment, an ability which was due to a flexible diet and new developments in family and social interactions.

Between 500,000 and 300,000 years ago, some of these developments became apparent. Humans began to build huts in open areas, covering them with branches and animal skins, or they used caves as their dwellings. They started to wear some type of clothing, learned how to keep a fire alive, and hunted in groups. A great deal of evidence for this has come from Africa. The new dwellings had resting areas and eating areas. There were areas for stone or woodworking, for meat cutting, and for food preparation.

Humans also invented mattresses and blankets. At Lazaret, near Nice, anthropologists found seaweed mattresses and wolf-pelt blankets in a dwelling that was 130,000 years old. Humans now used colouring materials, such as red ochre. Scattered finds also show a growing curiosity about shapes and design. All these developments suggest that humans were developing an artistic sense.

The Distribution of *Homo erectus*

The distribution of *Homo erectus* can be seen from the map (*above*) showing the main sites of fossil remains. *Homo erectus* was the only representative of humankind from 1,500,000 to perhaps less than 350,000 years ago. The passage from *Homo erectus* to *Homo sapiens*, like the passage from *Homo habilis* to *Homo erectus*, was very gradual. According to standards such as internal skull volume and size of the forehead, scientists estimate that *Homo sapiens* appeared on the earth about 350,000 years ago. Scientists do not know as much about the recent evolution of the large apes, but noteworthy is *Gigantopithecus*. This gorilla-like ape lived in China and India during the last million years and was perhaps the largest primate of all time.

HOMO SAPIENS

It is no longer possible to claim that the human species of the present time, which the scientist Carl von Linné named *Homo sapiens* in 1735, is completely different from the species *Homo erectus*. The physical, social, and cultural similarities between the recent human species are becoming more evident every day. Of course, *Homo sapiens* has undergone great changes in the last 150,000 years, particularly in the field of human culture.

The contribution of Africa in the development of the new human species was certainly of major importance. In fact, one of the oldest *Homo sapiens* fossil specimens was found in Africa. Some scholars consider this fossil, which was found at Broken Hill in Zambia, to be the last representative of *Homo erectus*. Beings of this group settled in southern Africa at least 120,000 years ago and lived there for many thousands of generations. The most complete skull was found in a cave in Zambia in 1921.

This human had a larger and more rounded head, a larger, already "modern" brain, and the protruding forehead bones typical of *Homo erectus*. The overall facial structure was rather delicate, showing the first hints of the smooth facial features that became typical of more recent human beings. For the first time, human teeth showed cavities. Through these developments, it is obvious that humans had begun to domesticate themselves. They had by now adopted the organized way of life that comes with culture.

Remains of *Homo sapiens* were found in eastern Africa as well as in the Far East, where the island of Java was an especially plentiful site. Individuals of the species *Homo sapiens*, with the same general features, also appeared in Europe and in the Near East. In the transition zones between *Homo erectus* and *Homo sapiens*, was the so-called subspecies of Neanderthals. For a while, these beings were considered a dead end in the evolutionary path. They were a type of *Homo sapiens* that fully developed around 80,000 years ago. The Neanderthals did not create artwork, such as statues and paintings on rocks, as their successors would. But they did develop a rich culture and complex religious rituals, such as burial ceremonies with offerings and flowers placed in pits with ochre-painted walls.

All evidence suggests that this species existed until about 40,000 years ago. At that time, *Homo sapiens* appeared, first in Asia (including Indonesia) and soon after in Europe. The great artists of the rock paintings belonged to this group. At this time, humans also reached Australia and North America. It seems probable that the human species evolved into several races as *Homo erectus* spread across the continents. Such a widespread division had not occurred before in the history of primates. Some scholars believe that this process took place on the various continents in parallel but independent ways.

The chart on the opposite page shows the physical evolution of the human group.

Homo sapiens pictured in a savanna landscape. Remains of this human were found at Broken Hill, Zambia.

Culture, the New Force of Evolution

Evolution involves the extinction of the species that are less fit for an environment and the development of new species that benefit from changes which occur in the environment. The progression from one species to another is not always a gradual process. Sometimes, it is more of a leap. The hominid *Homo* was the first being able to survive despite a lack of specialization. This defenceless, two-legged animal was easy prey for large carnivores. Yet it not only survived but spread all over the world. It survived because it developed culture (fire, language, toolmaking) which enabled its species to live anywhere on earth.

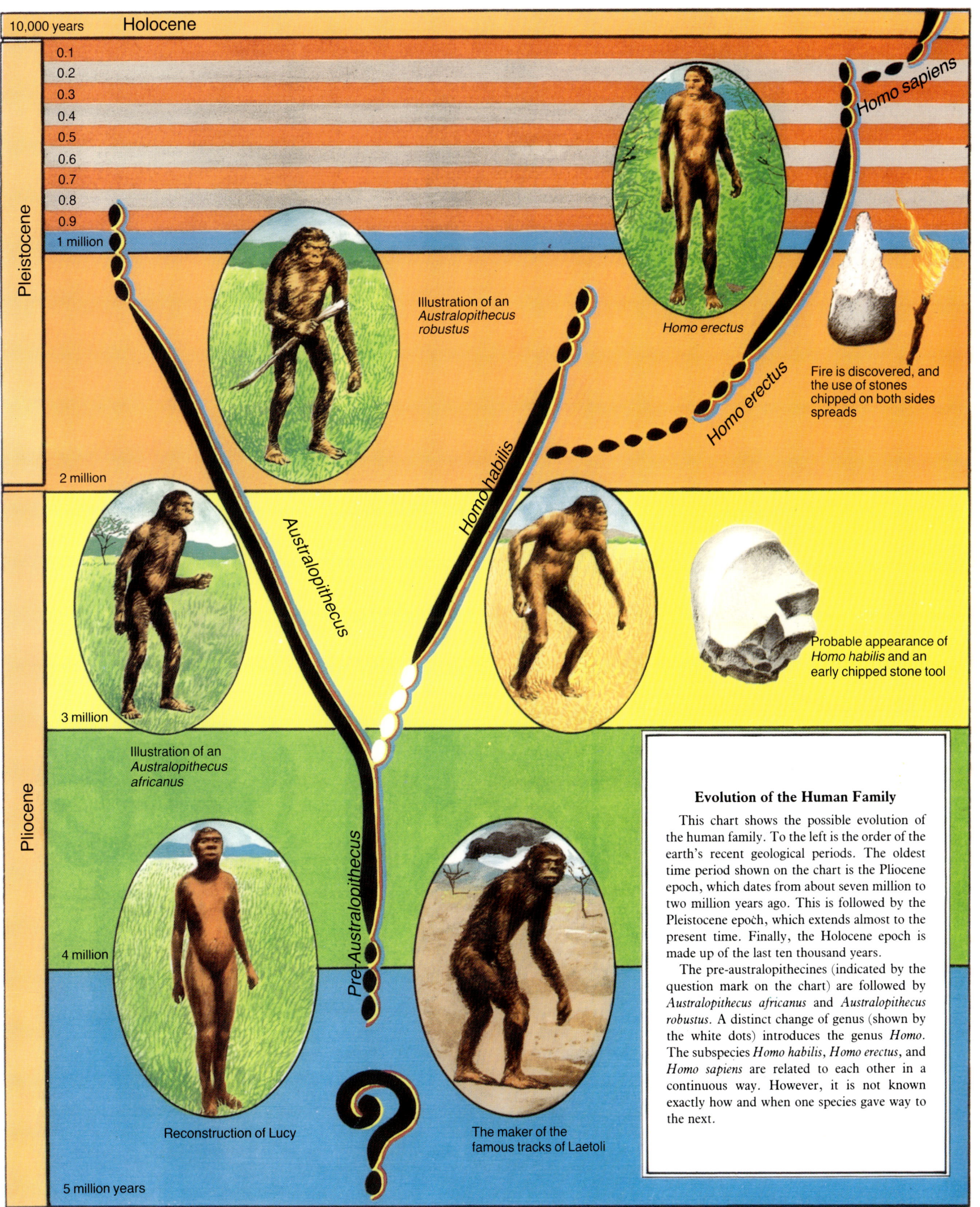

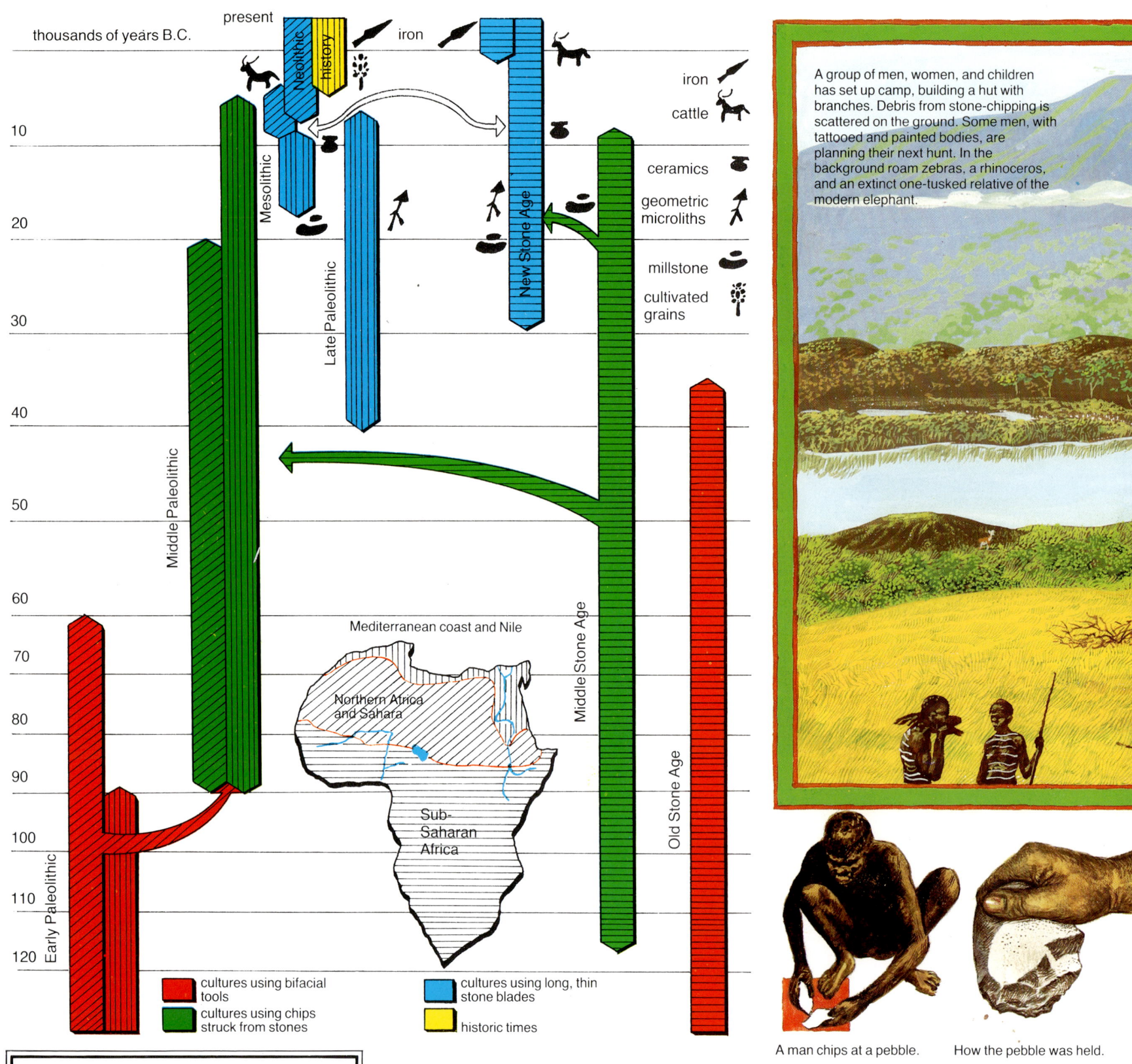

A group of men, women, and children has set up camp, building a hut with branches. Debris from stone-chipping is scattered on the ground. Some men, with tattooed and painted bodies, are planning their next hunt. In the background roam zebras, a rhinoceros, and an extinct one-tusked relative of the modern elephant.

A man chips at a pebble. How the pebble was held.

THE BIRTH OF CULTURE

The Evolution of Human Culture

Africa can be divided into three regions of human evolution: the area south of the Sahara, the Sahara, and the Mediterranean coast including the Nile valley. The societies in these areas had four stages of development. These stages were marked by: (1) the use of large bifacial tools; (2) the use of flake tools that were chips from stones; (3) the use of long, thin stone blades that were formed by striking a stone with another tool; (4) the development of herding and farming life-styles, the latter of which led to the invention of writing. The last stage was reached in very few places other than Egypt.

The essential characteristic of human beings is culture. Culture usually refers to the distinct patterns in which humans have conceived and expressed their lives in different regions and in different times. One expression of human culture is the way that they learned to change nature around them to survive. From the beginning, for example, humans lived in groups. These groups originally came together to survive, but they were kept together by shared experiences that gradually turned into the traditions and rules of culture.

The First Artifacts

The ability to adapt natural materials is important to developing a culture. Thus, in studying human culture, great importance is placed on stone artifacts. Individuals of the genus *Homo* were probably the first to learn how to break stones. The oldest-known artifacts are slightly older than two million years. They are chips (slivers) of quartzite or of other rocks of poor quality and are found in various sites in Ethiopia. Often the pebbles that were to be chipped were gathered in streambeds.

For a million years, the only remains found are broken pebbles, stones that had been used to hit the pebbles, and rough slivers used for cutting or scraping. In the oldest layer of the Olduvai excavation, six different kinds of tools were identified. The number increased to about a dozen in the following layer. Obviously, the toolmakers were striving to obtain a sharp edge on their stones, which were then used to tear flesh from the carcasses of dead animals or to cut hides or branches. Later on, the stones were cut to give two sharp edges that came together in a point.

The use of broken pebbles, also called the "culture of Olduvai," followed the expansion of the hominid populations throughout eastern Africa and into the neighbouring regions. This simple chipping method was occasionally used until the end of African prehistory.

Big-Game Hunting in the Savanna

The heavy, oval-shaped bifacial stones (chipped on two sides) were proof of the first attempts at balance and repetition of shape.

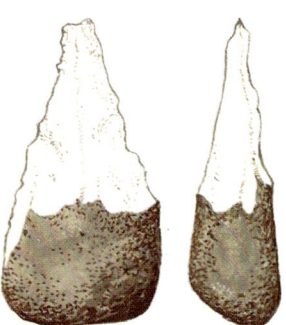
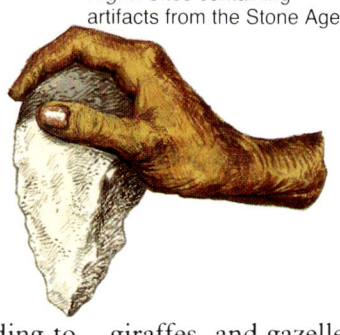
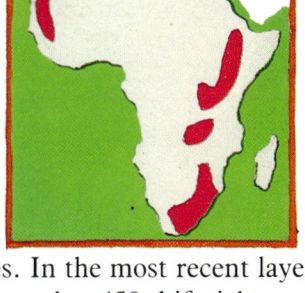

Two bifacials (*left*) found in the Olduvai Gorge. *Right:* A bifacial tool was held like this.

Right: Sites containing artifacts from the Stone Age.

The use of chipped stones varied according to changing needs. The cultures known for their use of bifacial tools, also called Acheulian cultures, corresponded to the development of *Homo erectus*. They first appeared around 600,000 years ago and settled in many regions of eastern Africa. During the following million years, these humans settled in clearings and river valleys throughout the savanna but kept clear of forests and deserts.

Big-game hunting in the savanna and on the rivers developed as a group activity and had an important effect on the culture. Some hunting areas were used for thousands of generations, and the prey were always the same: giant baboons, elephants, rhinoceroses, warthogs, giraffes, and gazelles. In the most recent layer of Olduvai, for example, 459 bifacials and polished knives were found together with a hippopotamus skeleton.

Hunting increased the importance of meat in the human diet. The use of fire, wood, and animal skins also became widespread, and the same sites were used as dwelling places for long periods. These new trends developed mainly during the late phase of the Acheulian culture, which flourished in various parts of Africa between 35,000 and 120,000 years ago.

Left: A stone point tied to a handle. *Above:* Four arrowheads with shafts. This new shape allowed different materials to be joined and increased the effectiveness of the tools.

The yellow area on the map (*top*) represents the Sahara region, inhabited by the Aterian hunters, during both dry and wet periods.

Tenere, a region of the Sahara, during a moderately dry period. Soon after a rain shower, a group of hunters is on the march, and one stops to drink from a puddle. Ostriches, which were common in the desert at this time, run in the background. African guinea fowl pick among the rocks in the foreground.

ADAPTATIONS TO THE SAHARA

North of the savanna territories is an area covered by scrub vegetation, called Sahel. Then the Sahara Desert begins. *Sahara* is an Arabic word meaning "a desolate land." The Sahara Desert covers one-third of Africa, has a diamond shape, and is located in the northern part of the continent. It is the largest desert in the world. It is a lowland stretching around massive central mountains and is crossed by isolated depressions, which are today filled with huge sand dunes. In the desert, there are high temperature swings in different seasons and between night and day.

The Sahara, which looks like an ocean of sand and rocks, has not always been like this. There have been periods when the Sahara region was even more hostile than it is today. But there were also periods when the land was watered by lakes and rivers and the plateaus were covered with mountain woods and grassy pastures. Of all the lakes, only Lake Chad still exists.

Animal and plant life flourished in the presence of water. Gazelles, antelope, hippopotamuses, rhinoceroses, warthogs, ostriches, and crocodiles inhabited the region. They formed the so-called Ethiopic fauna. In fact, the Sahara territory connected two regions which had different fauna: the Ethiopic region to the south, influenced by tropical savanna, and the temperate regions of Eurasia and the Mediterranean Sea. Saharan animals from the latter region were the donkey, the mouflon (a wild sheep), the wild ox, and the cat.

Human Settlements and Climate Changes

The late Acheulian hunters probably ventured into the Saharan grasslands during a rainy period between 100,000 and 130,000 years ago. Some came from the north, from the Maghreb region of North Africa. Others

Right: Chart showing changes in Africa's northern and eastern landscape over the last 100,000 years. In light blue, the increase and decrease of inland waters is shown. Brown marks the increase and decrease of desert land.

followed the Nile basin down from eastern Africa. They were big-game hunters and left traces of their presence around the various wet areas of the Saharan lowlands and even in the Tibesti Mountains. Around 90,000 years ago, the temperature began to drop, announcing the glaciation periods in the high latitudes. A cold, dry period followed, affecting the Sahara for at least twenty thousand years.

During this time, *Homo sapiens* spread along the Mediterranean edge of Africa. A group known as the Mousterians became dominant. These coastal peoples, who were of western Asian origin, fully adapted to the Mediterranean environment. They lived in the mountains on rocky hills covered with scrub along the course of seasonal streams. In this culture, the use of stone chip tools replaced the use of bifacials. The people learned how to attach stone tools to wooden handles and poles—an important invention for the time.

The Aterians

Around 70,000 years ago as glaciers retreated in the north, the Sahara regained some of its greenery, and humans again settled there. Along the Nile, human settlements were frequent. Here, the first exclusively Saharan culture began: that of the Aterians. The Aterians were aggressive, nomadic people who adapted to the environment of a changing semi-desert with wet and dry periods. Their own skills helped them to cope with these conditions. They made lances and harpoons with stone heads and knives with handles. They developed a flat chipping method to make larger, thinner tools of good quality. They also learned how to set ambushes for the herds of herbivores around their watering holes. The major concern of these people was control of their hunting territory.

The Sahara that the Aterians experienced had wooded mountains, stretches of heath, rivers, and small lakes in the depressions among the dunes. But the Aterians did not abandon the Sahara when it started to dry out once again around 40,000 B.C. For about twenty thousand years they coped with the desert. The changing environment simply increased their nomadic habits. It was the dramatic drought that took place between 20,000 and 10,000 B.C. that finally forced these skilled hunters and gatherers from the Sahara. Thus, the Aterian culture was extinguished.

The equatorial forest with Sango and Lupembia is marked in yellow on the map. The populations that lived in these regions during the Middle Stone Age were named after these two places.

THE DISCOVERY OF THE GREAT FOREST

The same adaptability that enabled the Aterians and other Paleolithic humans to survive in the desert led other groups to settle in Africa's many other environments. Within a short time, the hunters and food gatherers populated even the most hostile African environments. One of the last to be conquered was the equatorial forest. This environment's hot humid climate made adaptation difficult.

Humans faced the great African forest with a variety of tools. The smaller tools were used for cutting, scraping, or carving. Massive tools developed for heavy-duty work included large pointed pebbles, called peaks, that were sharpened on one side; bifacial axes made from elongated stones; rounded scrapers and planes shaped like a boat's keel; and spear heads. Many of these tools were held in the hand and were used to make other tools. In spite of rough appearances, these tools were the result of great progress. With them, humans had learned to make better use of the resources offered by the environments in which they lived.

Sangoans and Lupembians

The Sangoans were the first people to inhabit the African forests. They first left the wooded savanna for the forests about 50,000 years ago. But the complete conquest of the Zaire River basin, which occurred less than 35,000 years ago, is credited to later generations of the same population. These people were known as the Lupembians.

The forest people pushed their way north from the equator toward the Niger River. Their paths stop where the Atlantic savannas

A camp with crude huts made of branches stands in a clearing by a river in the equatorial forest of central Africa. The platforms on poles were used to keep food out of reach of animals.

Two stone bifacials, typical tools of these prehistoric people.

A woman comes back from the forest with food she has gathered using a stick with a stone point. Beyond her, a boy breaks open a termite nest with a digging stick to collect the grains stored by the termites.

were being replaced by the semi-desert Sahel and the Sahara desert beyond. Lance-shaped tools, similar to those of the Lupembians, have been found in Chad and in the central Sahara. These tools suggest the possiblity of contact between the forest peoples and the savanna peoples. Possibly, cultural exchanges were established between African and Mediterranean populations. The demanding environments of the equatorial forest and the Sahara produced some of the most highly specialized Paleolithic cultures known.

A Forest Culture

Very little is known about the life of the Sangoans and the Lupembians. The equatorial environment destroyed all evidence of them other than stone tools and traces of fire. These two illustrations attempt to picture what is known and to imagine what is not. Their groups often set up camp near a river and made use of all available resources. The large, spear-like blades were more often used as machetes than as lance heads. Some were tied to wooden poles and used to dig out roots or to break open termite nests. Plant material, especially wood, was probably widely used for daily tasks in various ways. It is thought that branches, bark, and vines were used to build temporary dwellings. A waterproof roof was necessary, at least during the rainy season.

The equatorial environments offered unlimited quantities of water, soil, and plant matter. The forest soil and underbrush offered all sorts of hidden foods to these gatherers. Women and children daily gathered these foods, which included roots, tubers, fruit, and insects. Both food and water were carried in bags, pouches, and containers made of bark, leaves, or animal skins. Here there was no need to search for food and water as in the savanna or in the desert. But the damp forest climate made storage of anything difficult, and food did not store well at all. It either had to be eaten right away or shared with a nearby family. Some attempts were made to preserve food by smoking it or roasting it. But even then the food had to be protected from wild animals. Often it was carefully wrapped and placed on platforms raised on stakes. Grains and nuts could be ground and stored. In the rain-drenched forest, tools made of wood or other plant materials eventually perished.

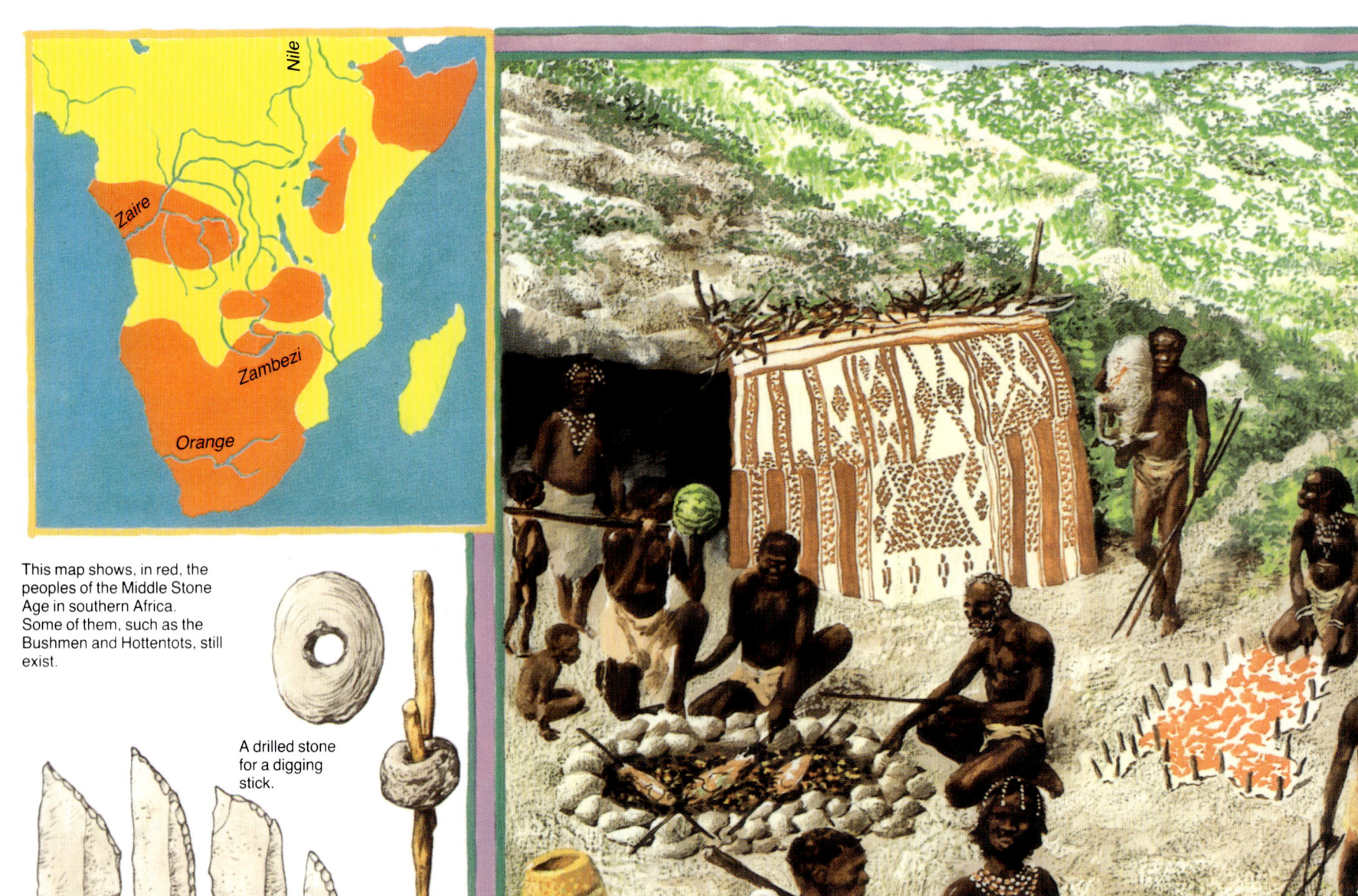

This map shows, in red, the peoples of the Middle Stone Age in southern Africa. Some of them, such as the Bushmen and Hottentots, still exist.

A drilled stone for a digging stick.

Microliths were mounted on handles and used to make other tools.

A digging stick fitted with a stone ring to increase the stick's weight and make the digging easier.

THE EXPANSION INTO SOUTHERN AFRICA

Exposure to new and constantly changing environments such as the desert and the equatorial forest changed life for Africa's Paleolithic populations and created new cultures. In eastern and southern Africa, however, the environment had been stable for many years. Thus, the populations tended to maintain their ancient life-styles. The land of the Acheulians, which was the open savanna, the grasslands, and the large tropical rivers with their pebbly beds, nurtured the culture of the large bifacials and cutting tools for a long time. However, in these regions, as well as in the steppes and mountains, some changes in traditions had begun.

In the process of stone chipping, humans started to create tools with definite shapes. For this purpose, a rough stone was pre-shaped before it was actually refined and the result was an oval stone. As the first rare bone tools appeared, people began to live in caves. At this time, the modern human species, *Homo sapiens*, appeared. All these events marked the beginning of the Middle Stone Age in South Africa. In some areas, the first hints of this period date back more than 170,000 years. Elsewhere, changes occurred after 40,000 B.C.

On the Mountains and Along the Coast

For over 100,000 years, the Acheulian way of life underwent changes before being replaced by modern cultures. The changes mentioned were seen mainly on the mountain prairies of the central African plateau and in the dry steppes of southern Africa. Similar changes took place on the plateaus of central-eastern Africa and extended to the mountains of Kenya and Ethiopia.

The Acheulian culture had also been changing and growing along the coast. Before this time, African settlements had always kept clear of the coasts and the ocean. But about 100,000 years ago, some groups began to settle along the coast of southern Africa. These people occupied caves and shelters under rocky outcrops and quickly learned how to use the sea's resources (molluscs, seals, seabirds). They also began the custom of leaving their dead inside caves, and this custom has preserved some human remains until the present

Fishermen and hunters settled along a stretch of southern Africa's coast, finding it rich in resources such as fish and game.

A man works on a rock-painting depicting a ceremonial dance. The oldest-known paintings from southern Africa are over 40,000 years old.

day. From such remains, scientists know that these people had a modern appearance and may have been the ancestors of the Bushmen who once populated all of southern Africa.

The Birth of Africa

Around 50,000 B.C., Africa's human populations were differentiating according to the different regions in which they lived. They became specialized in their environments, but at the same time, widespread changes were taking place. These changes led to the growth of the Stillbay-Pietersburg culture, which inspired the above illustration. Big-game hunting was generally abandoned, and a wider variety of animal and vegetable resources was used. In particular, people depended on a wide variety of animal species, hunting different species during certain periods of the year or within specific territories. Marine and freshwater animals also became an important food source. Most food, however, was the result of organized gathering in which all members took part.

It is thought that humans were not merely cooking their food but were also preparing it in varied ways. In the savanna, the first grinding tools appeared. The human communities began to interact with surrounding territories, and people lived at the same sites for an entire season or even for years. Shelters or huts with stone foundations were built in the open. Undoubtedly, the human population was rapidly increasing. But the success of the southern hunters and food gatherers is hard to explain if their intellectual and social achievements are not mentioned. These included strong family and tribal ties, a language which allowed humans to communicate with each other and to explain nature, and a complex collective memory expressed through myths.

The Rock Paintings

Humans with artistic capabilities have existed in Africa for more than 40,000 years. Rock paintings, which served as an expression of the human spirit, are evidence of this. The rock paintings depicted many characteristics of the Paleolithic culture, including ritual, myth, knowledge of the world, and society.

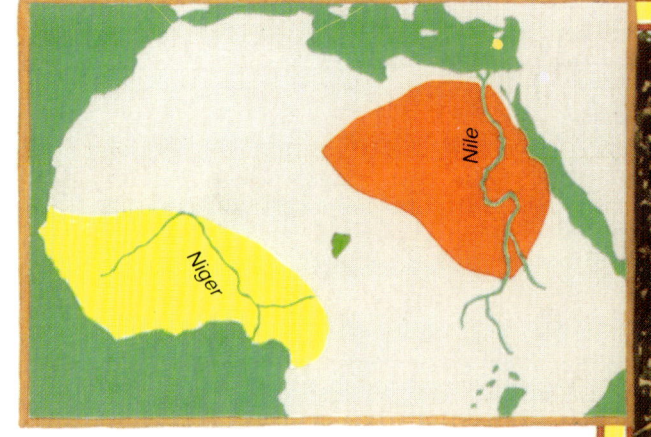

Settled societies of hunters and gatherers developed in the savanna and forest areas of Atlantic Africa (as shown in yellow). The Nile region (in red) was densely populated for the first time.

THE TRIBES OF THE NORTH

The African hunter-gatherers of the Recent Stone Age were also successful north of the equator. This success triggered an increase in population and in tribal conflicts. The New Stone Age developed in western and eastern Africa around 16,000 B.C. It is characterized by tools made of several parts (such as the bow), by microliths and blades of varying sizes, and by the plentiful use of vegetable foods. A similar development took place in the Mediterranean and Nile areas of the north. These cultures developed from late Paleolithic cultures of the Near East and from Mousterian populations who still lived along the edges of the Saharan desert. Unlike southern Africa and the savanna areas, however, changes in northern Africa broke with previous traditions. The Nile Valley, the Niger basin, and the Maghreb region offer interesting examples of such sudden changes.

Hunter-Gatherers Along the Nile

The harshness of the climate that stopped all life in the Saharan region around 20,000 B.C. also affected the Nile Valley. From 35,000 to 17,000 B.C., there is no trace of a human presence along the Egyptian stretch of the Nile. But humans continued to inhabit Nubia and the Sudan using flake tools, which were chips from stones. However, between 17,000 and 14,000 B.C., the use of stone blades began along the Nile, where some local groups began to resettle. This technique was also known at the northwestern end of Africa in the Maghreb region. Many characteristics connected the populations of these areas with those of the late Paleolithic age in Eurasia, such as the Palestinians in the Near East and the Iberians in Spain. Some scholars think there might have been communication between these cultures, both by land and by sea.

Vegetables were an important food source, and people began to depend heavily on certain plants. This was a first hint of the development of agriculture. Among the plants were wild barley in Egypt, and millet and sorghum in the Sudan region. The use of very small stone blades, called microliths, was prominent. By mounting microliths on arrows, harpoons, sickles, burins, drifts (boring tools), and graters, harvesting and grinding tools were made for the first time.

Around 10,000 B.C., massive flooding of the Nile announced the return of rainy conditions in northern Africa. Soon, rivers and lakes reappeared in the Sahara region. The microlithic culture spread across the Sahara and towards the Atlantic coast. In the Nile Valley, population boomed. The area soon swarmed with many small tribes. Many interesting cultures emerged.

Farmers in the West

Because of alternating dry-wet savanna and forest environments, the culture of western Africa developed in a different direction. About 12,000 years ago, the savanna was inhabited by groups using microlith knives. Later, in areas of dense vegetation, tribes of forest gatherers appeared. These people were using smooth stone axes for the first time. By around 4000 B.C., most of western Africa was connected to the central Sahara, and trade began. The Saharan people introduced ceramics and perhaps goat-keeping to the western regions in exchange for information on growing certain plants. Between 3000 and 1000 B.C., some plants, such as millet and sweet tubers, were probably grown in the Niger basin. By this time, settled communities throughout this area were producing part of their food by growing vegetables. They also kept goats and oxen.

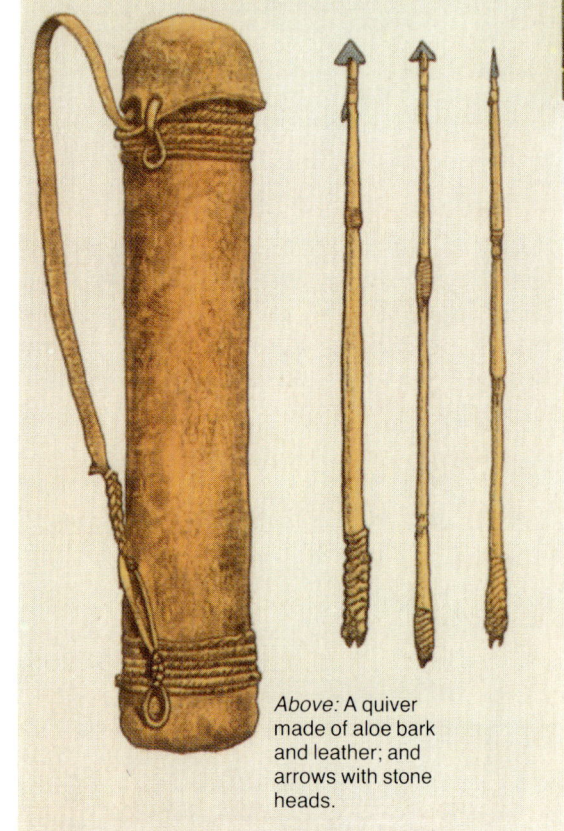

Above: A quiver made of aloe bark and leather; and arrows with stone heads.

Below: In the forests of western Africa, settlements became more stable and thus grew larger. Villages such as this one began to take shape. Here, a group of men drink palm wine.

In the Nile region, a group of archers attack a crowded campsite along the river. This illustration is based on findings from a group of tombs uncovered along the Nile, dating back to 12,000 B.C.

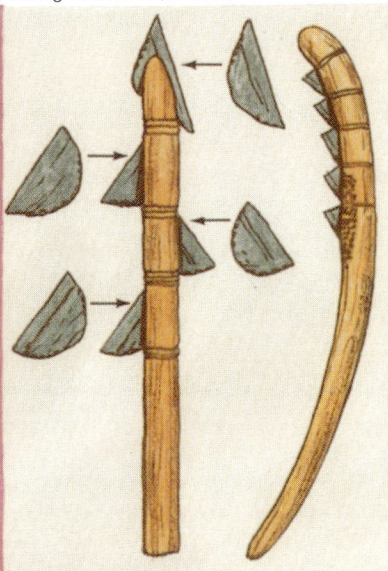

This sickle with microliths mounted on a wooden handle was used to harvest grain.

An arrow point made of microliths mounted on a wooden shaft (western Africa).

An Egyptian bas-relief shows a hut built on poles.

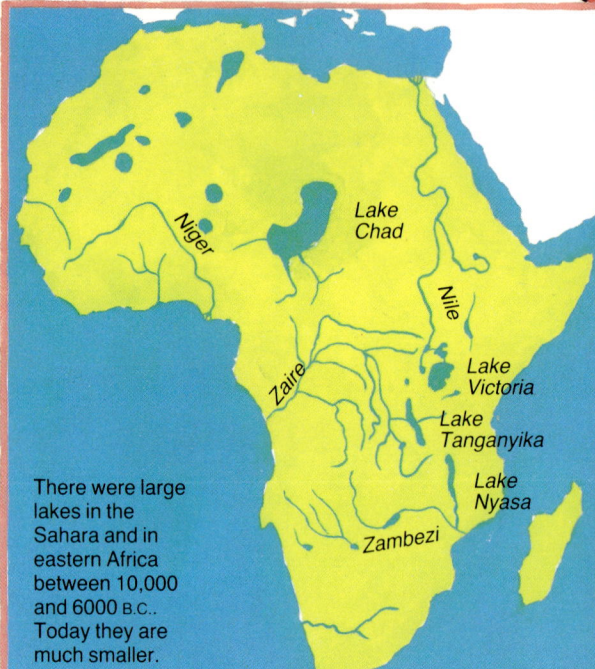
There were large lakes in the Sahara and in eastern Africa between 10,000 and 6000 B.C. Today they are much smaller.

Around 8000 B.C., the settlements around Lake Turkana became stable villages. The dwellings, which looked similar to those shown here, were sometimes elevated on piles to escape floods.

PEOPLE OF THE WATERS

Throughout Africa, lakes and rivers were plentiful around 10,000 B.C. The River Nile, in particular, fed by all its tributaries, had already become the great river it is today. The abundance of resources around the Nile probably caused overpopulation in the valley after 10,000 B.C. But this problem was widespread. Wherever inland waters were found, populations had developed. People in these settlements depended on the water resources to survive.

Around 9000 B.C., the Saharan rivers were already flooding, and the level of the lake waters was at a maximum. Lake Chad was eight times larger than it is today. The situation was the same in central and eastern Africa where countless lakes and wet areas were mixed with stretches of savanna. Until around 6000 B.C., when another dry period began, the wet Saharan region was an ideal environment for hunters, fishermen, and the first herders. This region was rich in wildlife, its hills were capped by Mediterranean woods, and its plateaus were covered by green prairies. Stretches of scrub or even sand dunes reminded humans of the desert nature of the region. But around the inland waters, life flourished.

The types of settlements were determined by the relationship between humans and water. Along the Nile, where flow varied, the human groups tended to gather in villages but were still very flexible. They wisely developed food resources both from the river and from the dry areas far away. The development of stable settlements and a life-style tied to seasonal changes spread elsewhere. Evidence suggests that great populations had developed along the northern coast. Communities stretched from present-day Mauretania to the Nile, and almost to Lake Victoria. These people fished and hunted near rivers and lakes. Fresh water was the key to life for many populations of this time, no matter where they were settled. Freshwater environments were rich in plant and animal resources, all of which

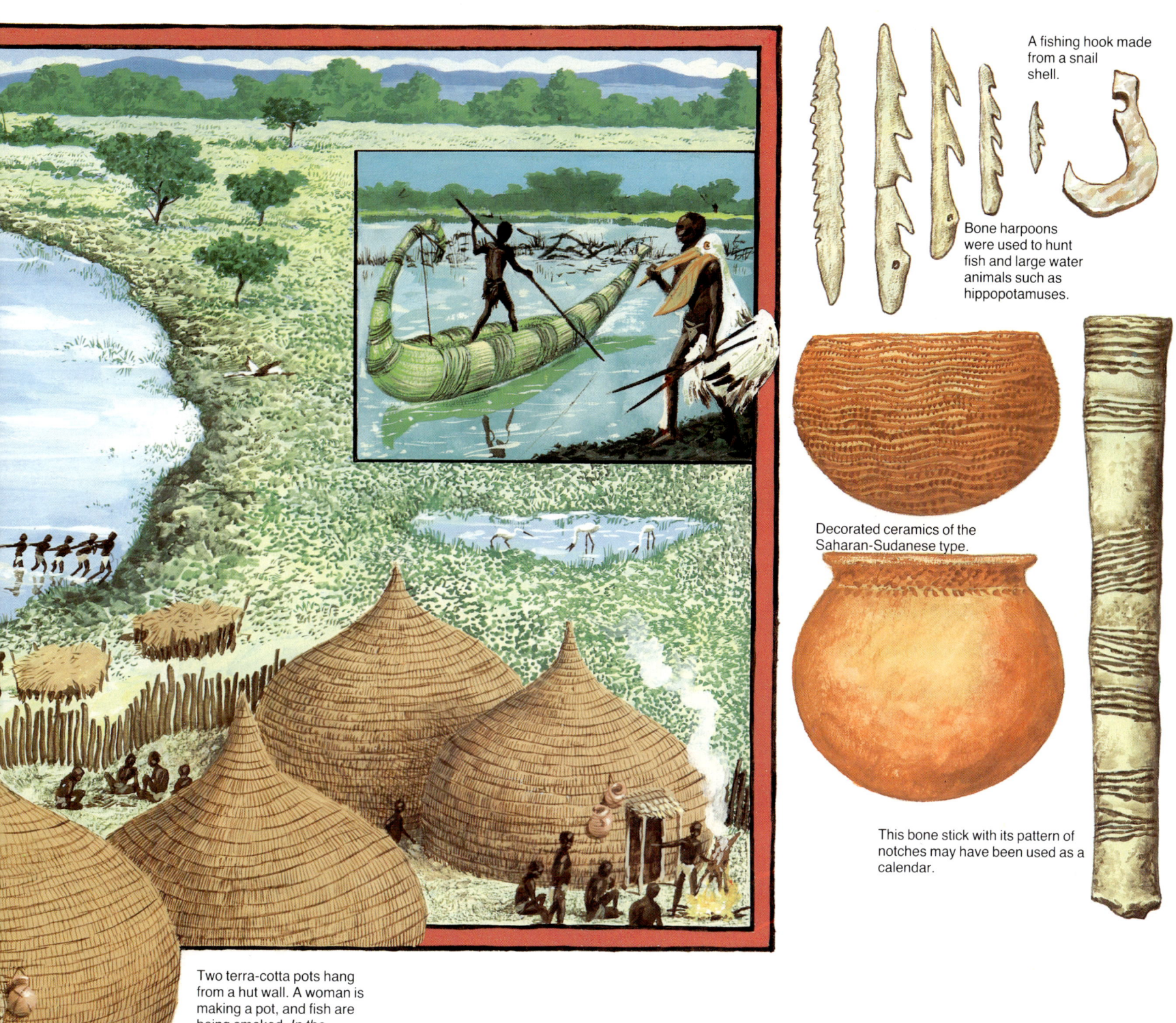

Two terra-cotta pots hang from a hut wall. A woman is making a pot, and fish are being smoked. *In the inserts:* Pictured are a hut built on piles (*left*), and a boat made of reeds and a hunter (*right*).

A fishing hook made from a snail shell.

Bone harpoons were used to hunt fish and large water animals such as hippopotamuses.

Decorated ceramics of the Saharan-Sudanese type.

This bone stick with its pattern of notches may have been used as a calendar.

were rapidly renewed. Fish were an especially good source of animal protein. As a result of the abundant resources, a way of life tied to water and fishing developed around many of Africa's lakes and rivers. This tradition was to last for a long time.

Achievements of the Culture

The expanding culture was evident by the material objects which represented it. There were elaborate weapons for hunting crocodile, hippopotamus, and turtle, as well as for catching large fish. Harpoons made of bone or tipped with microliths, and clubs were used by fishermen. Fish and shellfish were also preserved by smoking over fires. Sometimes, water and land snails were also part of the diet.

Unfortunately, many artifacts were made of perishable materials. Scientists will never have a glimpse of the boats, huts, wind shelters, or fences made with multi-coloured reed mats. Nor can they study the symbolic paintings on the bodies of men and women. Rock paintings, carvings, and other works of art supply our only information on this way of life. From them, we know that these peoples wore leather clothing. It is also known that they used nets and fish traps, and built small rush huts, baskets, and leather bags. They regularly used bows and throwing sticks for hunting.

The Discovery of Ceramics

Some of the most ancient ceramics in the world, dating back to 9000-8000 B.C., have been found in East Africa and the Sahara. Clay pots are decorated with patterns imitating baskets and carved gourds. The art of ceramics first appeared in cultures that had adapted to life near lakes, among peoples who were familiar with water and clay. This knowledge and a need to preserve and cook food led to the development of ceramics.

The life of nomadic shepherds on the Ahaggar plateau in what is now Algeria. To the left, terra-cotta pots are fired for use. Rock-painting was common (right) and new images were added to the rock-paintings each time the site was used. Decorated ostrich eggs (seen near the woman crouched on the ground) were used as containers.

THE BLOSSOMING OF THE DESERT

Around 2000 B.C., the climate of the Sahara turned dry again and the desert reappeared. It was the end of the world of the archers, fishermen, potters and seasonal gatherers. But while these people had developed a life-style tied to the water, other groups had remained close to the ancient way of life that was linked to the semi-desert areas, to the oases, and to the grasslands. These cultures marked the beginning of the Neolithic period.

The Neolithic Period in Africa

The Neolithic period centred on two or three regions of northern Africa, between 8000 and 4000 B.C. These regions were the high reaches of the Sudanese Nile, the Tener region in central Sahara, and the Algerian steppe. In Africa, the Neolithic period developed along different paths from those in Europe and Asia where plant cultivation was important. The idea of agriculture never reached many regions of the Saharan-Sudanese world, or perhaps it was rejected as it was in most of Africa.

In Africa, the Neolithic people specialized only in herding. Cattle herding was first practised in the central mountains and the Egyptian part of the Sahara. This herding life introduced a new factor of economic stability. It also encouraged mobility, with rhythms determined by the seasonal cycles, and where periods of settlement alternated with periods of nomadism (wandering). The Neolithic cultures in the scrublands of the Algerian Sahara kept goats and oxen, but only in small numbers.

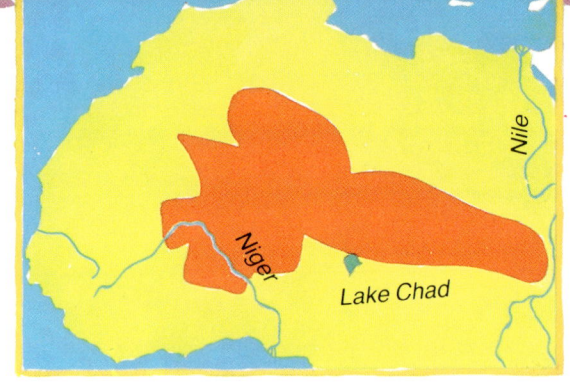

The expansion of the sheep-rearing Saharan-Sudanese Neolithic culture is shown in red on the map.

The Culture of Tener

The earliest known traces of domesticated herds are skeletal remains found in Egyptian oases, in Libya, and in the Tener region (dating from about 7000-5000 B.C.). Rock paintings from this period found on Saharan rocks also show evidence of this development. Herds of wild oxen and buffalo had roamed the Sahara for ages, but taming them must have begun just beyond the Saharan borders, perhaps in the vast grasslands of Egypt and the Sudan. The advantages of this technique were soon to be felt. The herd was a moving supply of fresh meat, milk, hides, fat, bones, and horns. Its size could be increased, creating "wealth" which brought social prestige to the herd's owner. Cattle-herding fitted especially well with hunting and gathering traditions in the Tener culture (5000-2000 B.C.) of the Saharan-Sudanese territories.

Society was divided into small bands of people in which males were dominant and people married within the tribe. The tribes were scattered over a variety of environments but were loosely held together by shared traditions. Their settlements of huts made of wood, reeds, reed mats, and hides have not been preserved to the present. Scientists have more knowledge of the shelters made in rocky areas. These shelters were often used by people and animals for generations. These peoples spent most of their lives in the open. Finds scattered over the desert include ceramic pots, arrowheads made of flint or quartz, grindstones, stone bowls, axes, and pestles sometimes shaped into animal forms. This skill in stone working, unparalleled in Africa, was the origin of the fine stonework of the Egyptian civilization.

First Signs of Agriculture

The earliest African peoples did not engage in farming. They lived by hunting and gathering, in close harmony with nature. Only later did traces of agriculture appear. In 6500 B.C., barley and wheat were grown in the Egyptian oases. In the Mauretanian Sahara, between 2000 and 1000 B.C., large communities grew wheat and millet, and built villages using stones and dry-wall techniques. In Ghana and Nigeria, the people grew millet and tubers by about 1500 B.C.

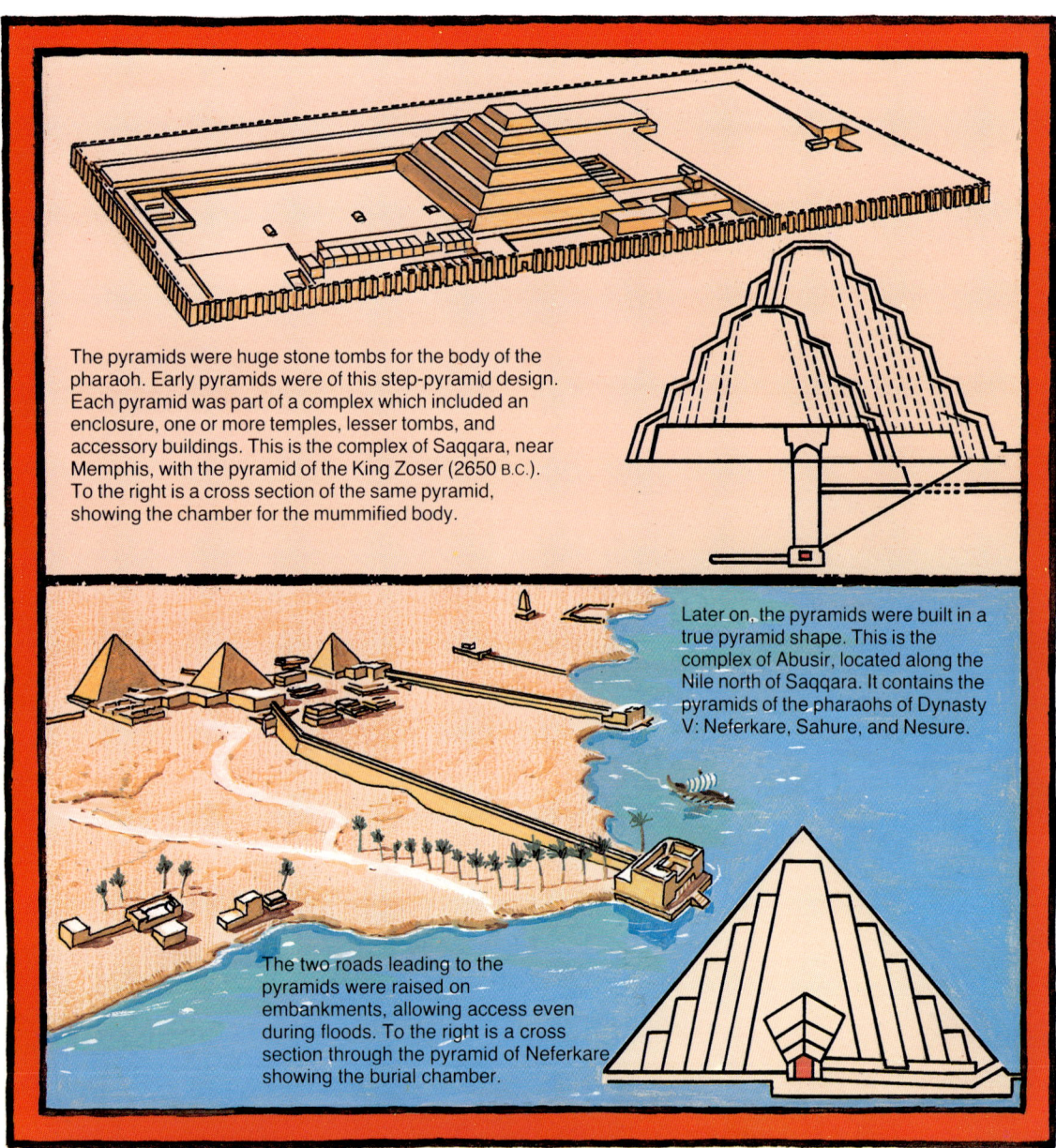

The pyramids were huge stone tombs for the body of the pharaoh. Early pyramids were of this step-pyramid design. Each pyramid was part of a complex which included an enclosure, one or more temples, lesser tombs, and accessory buildings. This is the complex of Saqqara, near Memphis, with the pyramid of the King Zoser (2650 B.C.). To the right is a cross section of the same pyramid, showing the chamber for the mummified body.

Later on, the pyramids were built in a true pyramid shape. This is the complex of Abusir, located along the Nile north of Saqqara. It contains the pyramids of the pharaohs of Dynasty V: Neferkare, Sahure, and Nesure.

The two roads leading to the pyramids were raised on embankments, allowing access even during floods. To the right is a cross section through the pyramid of Neferkare showing the burial chamber.

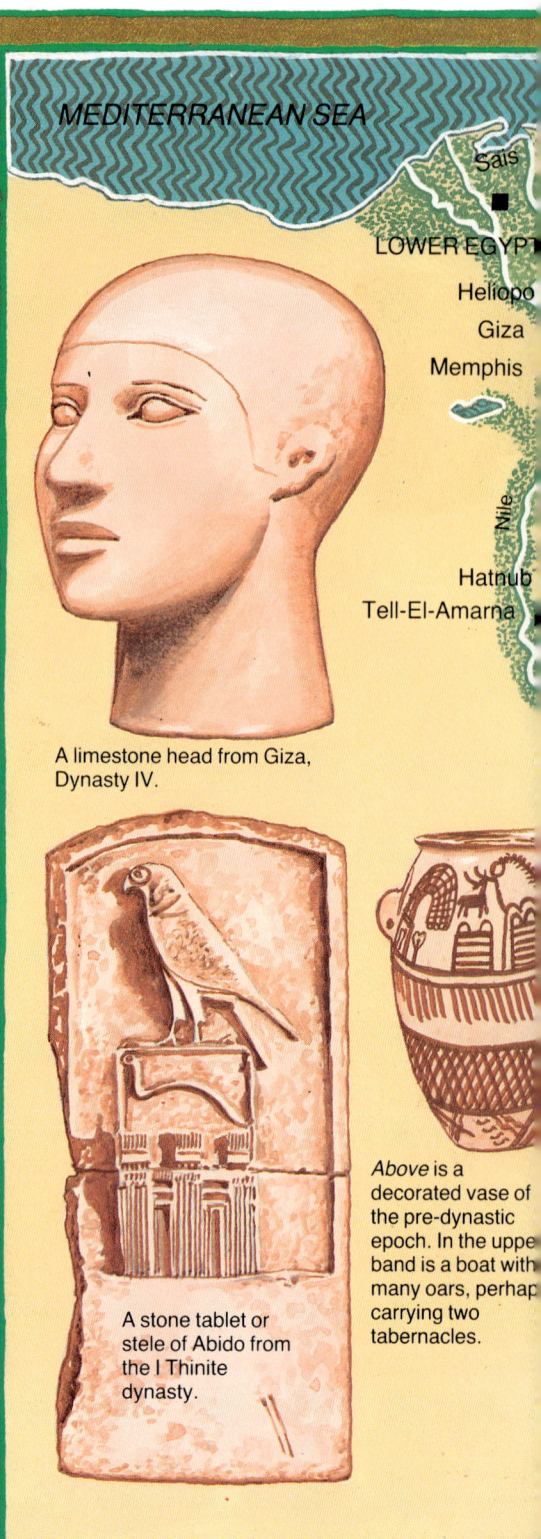

A limestone head from Giza, Dynasty IV.

A stone tablet or stele of Abido from the I Thinite dynasty.

Above is a decorated vase of the pre-dynastic epoch. In the upper band is a boat with many oars, perhaps carrying two tabernacles.

THE BIRTH OF EGYPTIAN SOCIETY

The Union of the Nile Valley

Along the fertile Nile Valley, the Neolithic period began around 10,000 B.C. Over the next seven thousand years, Egyptian civilization matured. The territory was divided into provinces called nomes, each of which was ruled by an appointed official, or nomarch. Between 4000 and 3000 B.C., the first kings appeared. There was the Kingdom of the Delta, in the north, protected by the god Horus, and the Kingdom of the Valley, to the south along the Nile, protected by the god Seth.

Around 3000 B.C., King Menes, a native of This, united the two kingdoms and created the town of Memphis at their meeting point. He began the Thinite epoch, during which the Egyptian civilization evolved. At this time, hieroglyphic writing was invented. This was a system of picture symbols used for formal writing such as official documents or religious carvings on temples or monuments. A simpler cursive writing, called hieratic writing, was invented for everyday use. A calendar with a year consisting of 365 days was invented.

Between 1550 and 1300 B.C., the king came to be called pharaoh. The pharaoh, sovereign of the two kingdoms (the Delta and the Valley), wore a dual crown, a symbol of the two protector gods. He was believed to be the god Horus in human form. Both pharaohs and gods needed perfect dwellings to symbolize their power. For this reason, palaces, temples, and royal tombs were built.

The Old Kingdom

After the two kingdoms united, a period of great prosperity began in Egypt. This period, known as the Old Kingdom, lasted for four dynasties. The first of these was Dynasty III ruled by King Zoser. He accomplished great architectural works, recognized the importance of writing, and turned the cult of the sun god Re into a cult of the king. The priests of this cult, which was based in Heliopolis, were

The Dynasties

Since monarchy was the centre and the heart of Egyptian life, the Egyptians marked their history by the order of the royal dynasties. This method is still used today to define the various periods of ancient Egyptian civilization.

THINITE EPOCH 3000-2660 B.C.
Dynasties I-II

OLD KINGDOM 2660-2180 B.C.
Dynasties III-VI

FIRST INTERMEDIATE PERIOD 2180-2040 B.C.
Dynasties VII-X

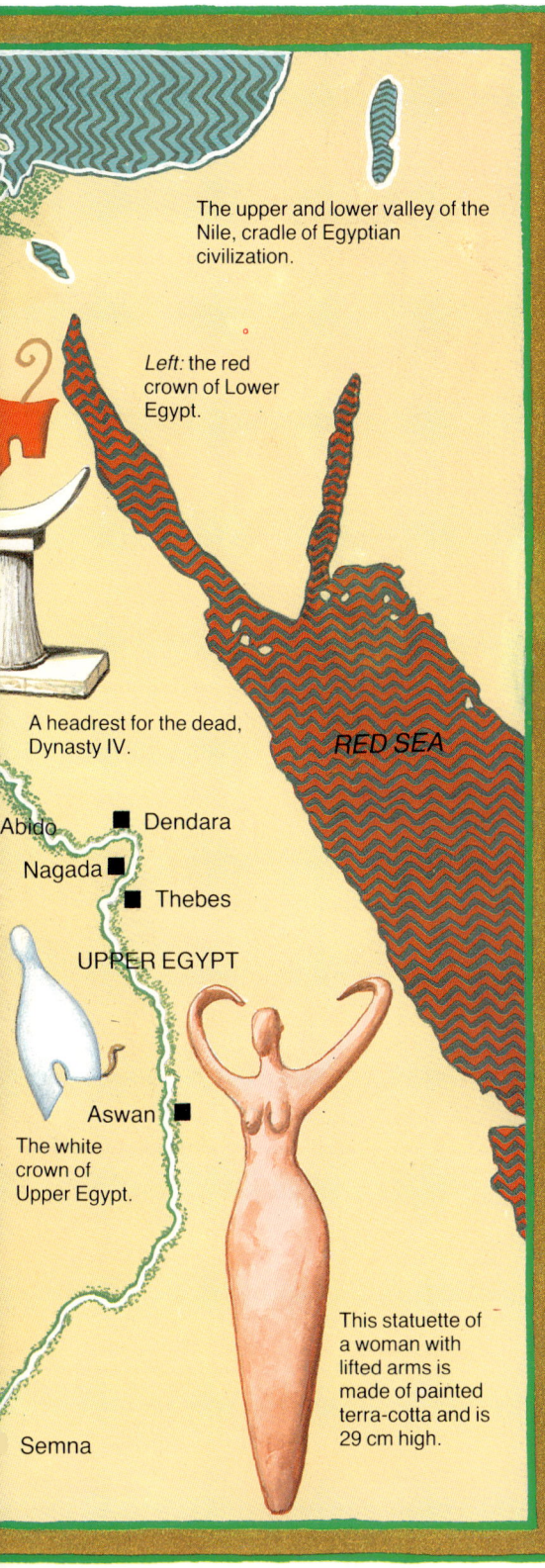

The upper and lower valley of the Nile, cradle of Egyptian civilization.

Left: the red crown of Lower Egypt.

A headrest for the dead, Dynasty IV.

RED SEA

Abido
Dendara
Nagada
Thebes

UPPER EGYPT

Aswan

The white crown of Upper Egypt.

Semna

This statuette of a woman with lifted arms is made of painted terra-cotta and is 29 cm high.

MIDDLE KINGDOM 2040-1780 B.C.
Dynasties XI-XII

SECOND INTERMEDIATE PERIOD 1780-1560 B.C.
Dynasties XIII-XVII (period of the Hyksos)

NEW KINGDOM 1560-1070 B.C.
Dynasties XVIII-XX

THIRD INTERMEDIATE PERIOD 1070-713 B.C.
Dynasties XXI-XXIV

LAST DYNASTIES 713-332 B.C.
Dynasties XXV-XXX

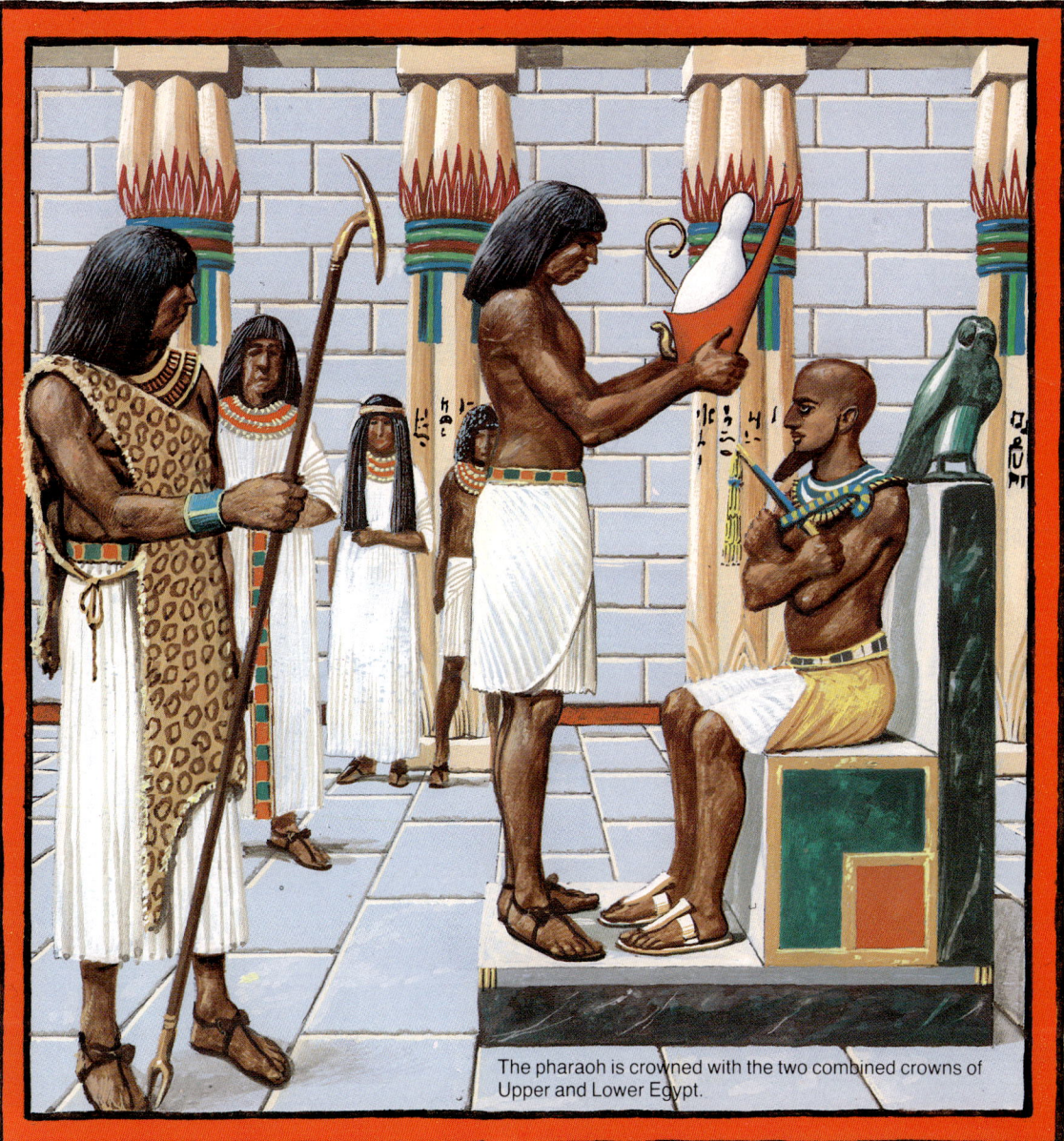

The pharaoh is crowned with the two combined crowns of Upper and Lower Egypt.

prominent and powerful in Zoser's reign.

People of Dynasty IV built the pyramids of Giza, Meidum, and Dahshur. Each pharaoh had his own pyramid, and each pyramid was surrounded by other lesser ones that hosted the other members of the royal family. Also during this dynasty, the first cadastres (records of land owned by the pharaohs or by individuals) were compiled, currency was introduced, and schools for scribes (administrators) were founded.

By Dynasty V, gold became the currency of trade, and Egyptian commerce expanded into the Mediterranean world. The empire was at its height and exercised great influence in the Middle East. But during this time, the pharaoh's power lessened as priests and government officials fought for control. Also, a nobility class appeared, which included princes, relatives, and the faithful followers of the pharaoh. Dynasty VI introduced a period of corruption that eventually caused the fall of the Old Kingdom. The power of the noble landowners, social unrest, and invasions by desert nomads all contributed to this fall.

Hieroglyphic Writing

The most ancient form of Egyptian writing is hieroglyphic writing in which pictures represent ideas and sounds. When hieroglyphic writing was replaced by another writing system in the first few centuries A.D., the meaning of the hieroglyphs was forgotten. But the discovery of the Rosetta stone in 1799 helped scholars to decode this writing. Found near the Nile River, this stone tablet had three inscriptions on it—one in Greek, one in Egyptian, and one in hieroglyphic writing. The French scholar Jean François Champollion decoded the stone's hieroglyphs in 1822.

Egyptian farmers at work. In the foreground, grain is being threshed; behind, harvesting takes place; in the background, workers measure the fields and pick vegetables.

An Egyptian hunts birds in a swamp, accompanied by a woman, child and pet cat. The boat is made of papyrus stems and the hunters are using boomerang-like throwing sticks as weapons.

EVERYDAY LIFE IN EGYPT

The Nile, Source of the Egyptian Miracle

Life in Egypt depended on resources from the land. Egypt was an oasis in the desert, which had been made fertile by the yearly floods from the Nile and by constant irrigation. From July to September the waters of the Nile, loaded with silt and plant debris, flooded the valley and left fertile soil that could yield two to three harvests a year. In November and December, after the waters had retreated, the soil was ploughed with small ploughs and seeded. In Egypt, barley, wheat, and flax were cultivated, as well as numerous fruits, including date palms, fig trees, and grapevines.

Domestic Animals, Hunting, and Fishing

Since Dynasty I, farmers had been keeping cattle, sheep and goats. They even tried to domesticate wild animals such as gazelle. Some people kept bees as early as Dynasty V. The honey was used as food and in the manufacture of perfumes and cosmetics; beeswax was used in perfumes, in the mummification process, and for paintings. Wild animals were hunted along the river with the aid of traps, nets, bows and arrows, and even trained dogs. Fish were caught with lines and various kinds of nets.

Towns and Landed Properties

From the time of the Old Kingdom, towns had become important, especially in the Delta region. They were centres of trade, oriented towards the Mediterranean and the Middle East. They were populated by merchants, shipowners, sailors, and artisans such as brickmakers, masons, carpenters, sculptors, tanners, weavers, and potters.

Around the end of the Old Kingdom, "landed" properties appeared. These great estates were self-sufficient and ruled by the nobility who owned them. They included a marketplace, peasant farmers and artisans. The property owned by the priests around the temples was also organized in this way. Towns and landed estates were in competition with each other but managed to maintain the balance and prosperity of the country.

The Priests

The priests were not spiritual guides for the people. They were the servants of the god whose presence in the temple was denoted by a statue. The main task of the priests was to care

Artisans at work in an Egyptian town busy with their carpentry, spinning and weaving, and pottery making.

for the temple statue. They were also in charge of organizing the temples and all related business: administration, taxes, and religious practices.

Officials and Intellectuals

In Egypt there was growing tension between the power of the divine pharaoh and that of the local nobility. To maintain control, the king needed the aid of a powerful group of officials. Among them were the vizier (the head of justice and administration), police and tax officers, chancellors, directors of public works and of transport, and local administrators. Most influential were the scribes, who knew the secret of writing. They formed the intellectual class and provided Egypt with its literature.

The Political and Social Structure in Egypt

PHARAOH
The divine king of Egypt to whom the gods had bestowed power over the earth and all humankind

PRIESTS
Devoted to the cult of the god statues in temples

VIZIER
Linked the pharaoh to the administration

ARMY
Formed by local troops, later also by foreign mercenaries

COURT NOBILITY AND HIGH OFFICIALS
Performed administrative tasks and also owned private land, separate from the pharaoh's possessions

SCRIBES
Belonged to educated class and were distributed throughout the system, even to the village level

MERCHANTS, SHIPOWNERS, SKILLED PEOPLE
Independent, mainly active in the Delta towns

FREE ARTISANS
Lived and worked in the towns

FREE FARMERS
Landholders and labourers

SUBJUGATED ARTISANS
Worked in workshops of the pharaoh, of the high officials, and in the temples

SUBJUGATED FARMERS
(peasants)
Worked the land of the pharaoh, of the officials, and of the temples

PRISONERS OF WAR AND SLAVES
Subject to the pharaoh, the court, and the high officials

THE MIDDLE AND NEW KINGDOMS

The Middle Kingdom

After the end of the Old Kingdom, Egypt experienced a long period of disorder. Toward the end of this period, the princes of Thebes declared themselves the kings of Lower and Upper Egypt and founded Dynasty XI. Thebes was the empire's new capital. In 1991 B.C. a vizier named Amenemhet seized the throne and founded Dynasty XII. This was the beginning of the Middle Kingdom.

During the Middle Kingdom, Egypt experienced two centuries of prosperity and cultural flowering. One centre of this activity was the second cataract of the Nile. To the east, the Sinai route was under its protection. A sea route was opened across the Red Sea to the land of Punt, and relationships with the Aegean world and with Phoenicia were begun.

At the end of Dynasty XII, another period of corruption and weak rule began. Eastern people known as Hyksos ("foreign rulers") spread throughout the country. These invaders seized control, proclaimed Tanis their capital, and ruled for about one hundred years. From them, the Egyptians learned about horses, chariots, and other weapons.

its power between 1463 and 1380 B.C.

An exchange of art and increasing trade brought Egypt great wealth. The period was characterized by the construction of huge temples. For example, Amenhotep I chose a new burial site for the kings. This was the Valley of the Kings, near Thebes. Queen Hatshepsut also built a magnificent temple. The royal tombs were decorated with incredible splendour. They contained furniture, jewels, and cosmetic items.

The pharaoh Amenhotep IV (also called Akhenaton) introduced a new religion of the

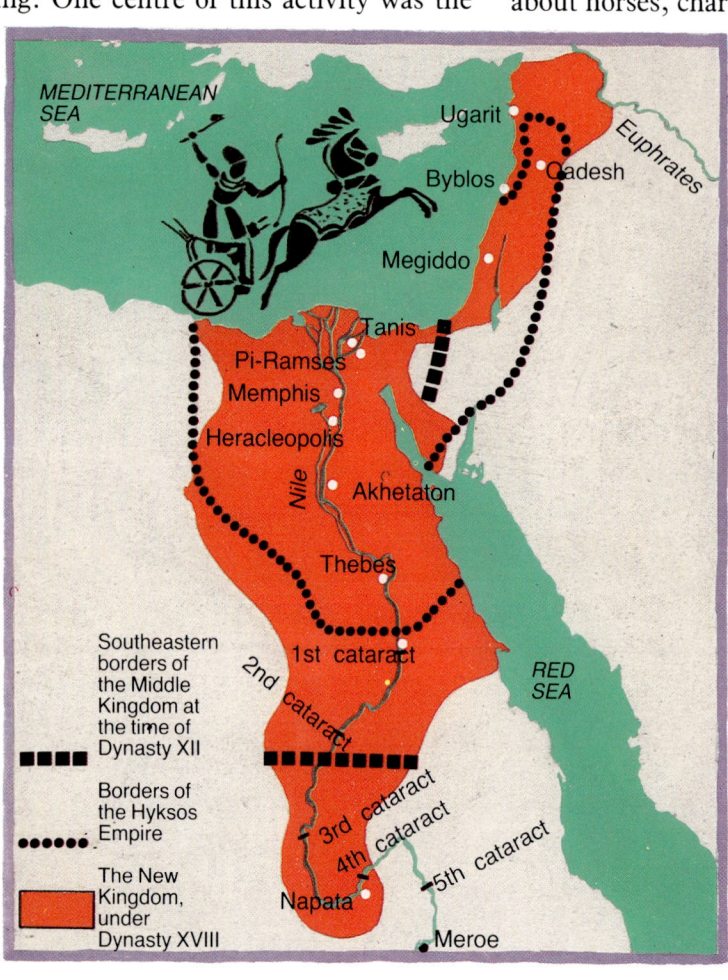

In red, Egypt during the Middle and New kingdoms.

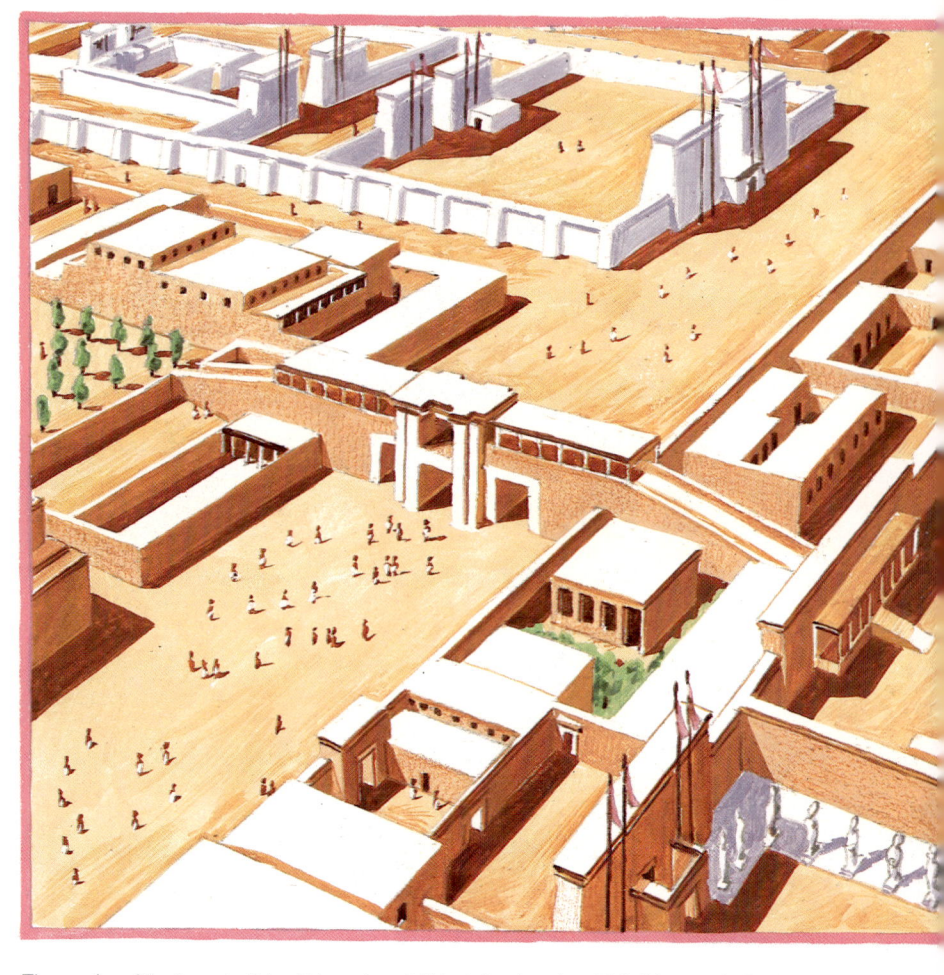

The centre of the town built by Akhenaton at Akhetaton (modern Tel el Amarna). On the right is the palace of the pharaoh. To the left are the official quarters. On ceremonial occasions, the pharaoh would appear before the people, who crowded into the loggia that crossed the street to see him.

oasis of Fayum, where the pharaohs of Dynasty XII lived. Due to a skilful irrigation system and an influx of new people, Fayum became the most active region in Egypt. It was a major cultural centre, where important religious and literary texts were written. Throughout Egypt, the construction of temples and pyramids resumed.

Egypt too began to expand during this time. The army formed for this purpose also proved useful for protecting the country against attacks from Asia and Libya. Egyptian territory soon extended south all the way to the

The New Kingdom and the Restoration of Unity

Under Dynasty XVIII, native Egyptians drove the invaders out of the country and reunited Egypt. In the period which followed, known as the New Kingdom, Egypt became a powerful empire and an important force in Middle East politics. Its strength came from its army. With iron swords, chariots, horses, and military techniques introduced by the Hyksos, Egypt's army conquered various Middle East territories. The empire reached the height of

sun god Aton. His religious changes are said to have been one cause of the cultural growth, but they also caused much unrest among the people. Akhenaton also built a new capital at Akhetaton about 300 kilometres from Thebes. Later the capital was moved back to Thebes.

The real crisis of the period was caused by great migrations of Assyrians, Achaeans, and various "sea peoples" entering the Delta. Power struggles and economic and religious problems resulted from these invasions and brought about the end of the New Kingdom.

The rocky approach to the Valley of the Kings.

Chamber of the sarcophagus in the tomb of Nefertari, Valley of the Queens, Dynasty XIX.

The region of Luxor and Thebes (Karnak is the name of the Arabic village built on the location of ancient Thebes), showing the Valley of the Kings and the Valley of the Queens.

The Valley of the Sphinxes is in Luxor. The sphinx, an animal with a lion's body and a man's or a god's head, represented the power of the pharaoh or of the god.

Valley of the Kings
Passage to the Valley of the Kings
tombs
Temple of Hatshepsut
Tombs of the Nobles
Valley of the Queens
tombs
Temple of Ramses II
Palace of Amenhotep
Temple of Ramses III
Temple of Seti I

Two papyrus-shaped columns in a room of the great temple of Luxor.

Nile

Karnak
Temple of Amon

Processional way of the sphinxes

Thebes

Great temple
Luxor

north

0   1,000 m

A portion of a pectoral plate (*above*), found in the tomb of Queen Aahhotep in Dira Abu'n Naga. It depicts a scene of regal purification.

The great burial temple of Queen Hatshepsut, Dynasty XVIII.

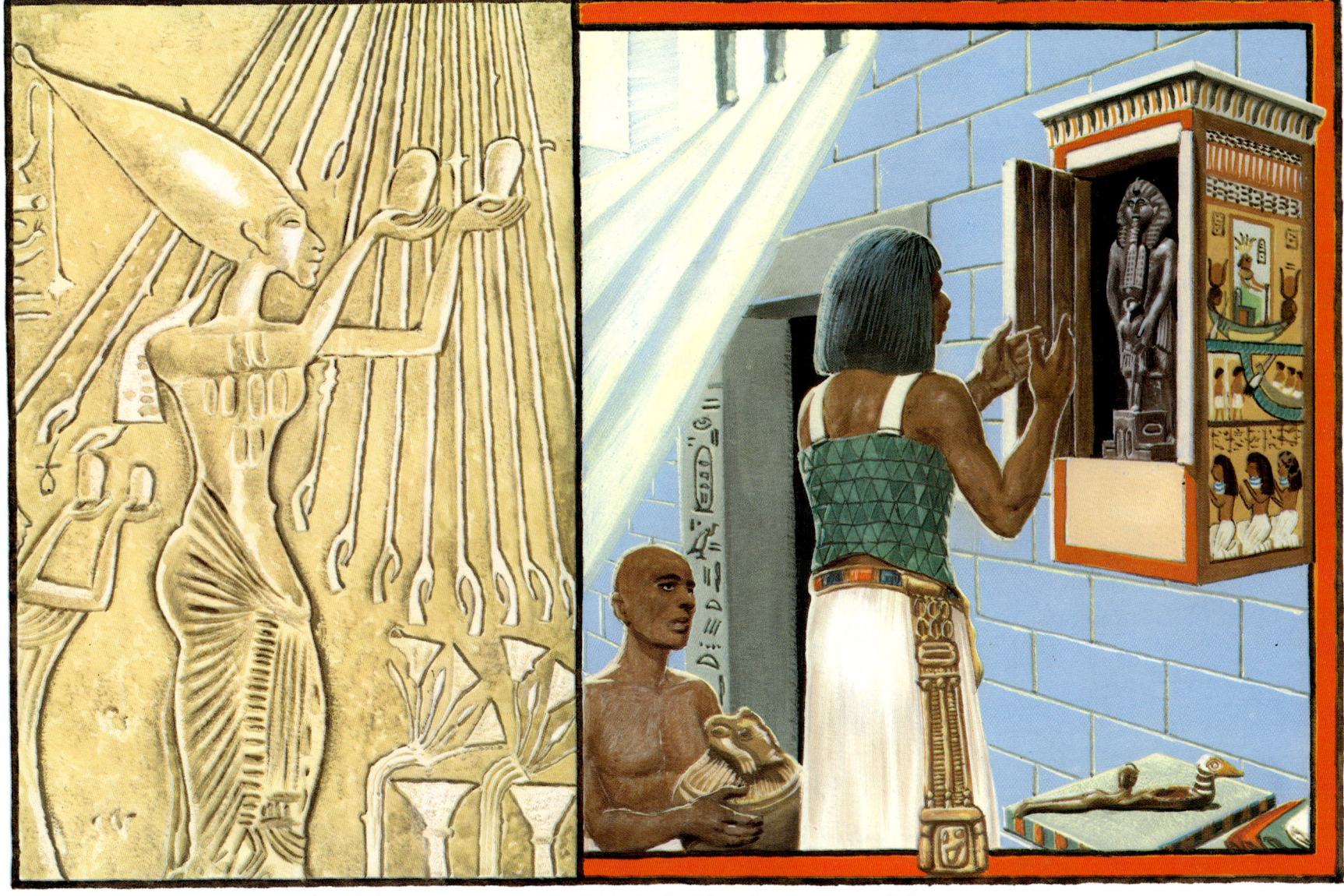

The Pharaoh Akhenaton and Queen Nefertiti behind him make an offering to the sun god, whose beneficial rays are depicted in the shape of divine hands.

Celebrating the divine cult: a priest is seen with the statuette of the god in the temple.

The god Horus

The god Thoth

The goddess Hator

The goddess Isis

THE EGYPTIAN RELIGION

The Gods of Egypt

The Egyptians believed that gods and goddesses affected every aspect of life. Human existence depended on these various deities. The gods were protectors of right, justice, and life in the earthly world as well as in the underworld. They were considered the incarnation of power, and the symbol representing them in official writing was a royal sceptre. But various animal shapes or shapes that were a human-animal mix were used to represent specific deities. All of them were incarnations of divine power. These figures were given names; thus each deity had its own identity and specific character.

All the gods were created by an original god. The original god, however, was not the same throughout the different periods. Ptah of Memphis "produced the gods," while Amon of Thebes "produced gods and man." Differences such as this explain the development of local gods. Each Egyptian city had a special god to whom the people prayed in addition to the major deities.

Starting about 2000 B.C., religious writings, as well as hymns and rituals, were produced within the royal palace and the great temples. The religious scholars studied the nature of the gods and would determine the gods' shapes and images. There were at least three great Egyptian schools of religion: the school of Memphis, centred on the god Ptah; the school of Heliopolis, based on Aton-Re, the father god of the eight main gods; and the school of Hermopolis, based on the god Thoth, the judge.

The Cult of Aton, The Sun God

The pharaoh Amenhotep IV, as mentioned earlier, devoted himself to the sun god Aton. Amenhotep was convinced of the existence of this one god and began major religious reforms, backed by Queen Nefertiti and the

Accompanied by priests and dancers, the processional boat of Amon is carried out along the way of the sphinxes at the temple of Karnak.

priests of Heliopolis. In his reforms, he named Aton as the sole god and suspended the worship of the god Amon and most other gods. In his devotion, Amenhotep changed his name to Akhenaton, which means "he who is appreciated by Aton." These changes angered many people, especially the priests of the god Amon. In reaction, the pharaoh ordered that all the statues of Amon be destroyed and that his name be eliminated. The pharaoh's dream was that all people would live in peace and prosperity under the protection of Aton, who was the god of all people, not only of the Egyptians. Akhenaton's reform lasted only for his lifetime. After his death, Egypt returned to the traditional religion. During Dynasty XIX, all the cults were resumed, the temples and statues were restored, and the priests gained new importance.

The Religious Rituals

As the chief priest of Egypt, the pharaoh's task was to build temples, which were the dwelling places of the gods. He also had to perform the daily rituals. Since the pharaoh could not perform the rituals in each temple, priests were also given the power to perform these rituals. The daily ritual centred on the statue of the main deity. Each morning the priest would enter the temple and purify it with fire and incense. He then broke the seal on the door of the sanctum, to shed light on the god's face. The priest would then sing a hymn, rub the statue with ointment, and embrace it. Offerings of food, incense, and perfumes followed. The ritual ended by washing the statue. An evening ritual prepared the deity for its night rest.

The people could not enter the temple. They could honour the god only during special celebrations for which they gathered in the temple courtyards. The priests carried the god on a processional boat. As the statue passed, the people greeted it with songs and shouts.

The god Amon-Re

The god Osiris

The god Ptah

The god Anubis

The god Khnum

Shown above is a cross-section of the tomb of an artisan at Deir-El-Medina. The mummy was placed in the crypt beneath the chapel.

The ceremony of the opening of the mouth allowed a mummy to resume eating and thus come back to life. After purifications and sacrificial offerings, a priest read the text of the book of the dead. Meanwhile, another priest opened the mouth of the mummy using a special tool.

HUMANITY'S PLACE IN THE UNIVERSE

The Creation of Life and the World

The Egyptian people were very interested in the origin of life and the world. The central point of Egyptian religious thought was that creation was the work of a god. The three schools of religion believed in a creator god although the creator himself did not exist on earth. Their faith said everything that existed had to originate in the god's heart. He had put order into the universe by means of eight principal gods.

For the school of Memphis, the creator was the god Ptah, who had put order into the universe and into Egypt. For the school of Heliopolis, the sun god Aton-Re was the creator of the world and the father of all other gods. According to the school of Hermopolis, the eight gods were created by Thoth. Thoth also created an egg from which the sun emerged. In all three schools, the basic idea was that creation was a sacred act from which life emerged. For this reason, life was considered sacred and the act of creation had to be re-enacted every day. The daily rise of the sun was repetition of the creation. The pharaoh's task was to maintain the universal balance, allowing the sun to rise and assuring life for all beings.

The concept of life was the centre of Egyptian faith. Egyptians loved life and did all they could to preserve it. Their joy in life was evident in their architecture, art, myths, and tales. The same joy is also found in the decorations of temples and tombs, and on the columns of their monuments.

The Survival of the Pharaoh

The royal funerary texts of the Old Kingdom, called *Texts of the Pyramids*, dealt with the pharaoh's fate and described his life in the other world. According to these texts, the dead ruler would fly up to the sky to become a star, or to accompany the god Re in his solar journey. According to other texts, the king would become the god Osiris and be given eternal life by the mummification ritual. The ceremony of opening the mummy's mouth was also supposed to bring life after death.

The search for life after death became a concern of the entire population in the Middle Kingdom. Mummification and survival rituals were no longer performed only on the pharaoh's body. Tombs became more and more numerous, containing even artisans and workers. Coffins also became more common.

The Depiction of Eternal Life

An ancient depiction of life after death shows a deceased person seated at a table, eating. Eternal life was thought to be a continuation of earthly life. For this reason, the tombs were filled with food and offerings.

A granite sarcophagus of a royal scribe shows him dressed in the clothing of the living at the beginning of Dynasty XX, around 1300 B.C.

Ankh

The falcon Horus carries the "Ankh," the symbol of life. This symbol is ancient, and its origins are mysterious.

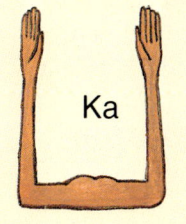

Ka

Ba

Akh

The Egyptians believed that humans resulted from the interaction of three elements: "Akh," the divine power; "Ka", the life force which, like a breath coming from the god, sustained the living being; and "Ba," the personal conscience of each person. The union of Ka and Ba formed the human spirit. When Ka departed from the body, death occurred.

Djed

The "Djed" pillar (here surmounted by the symbol of life and by the sun Ra) was a reminder of the backbone of Osiris, which was broken during his death and restored through resurrection. It symbolizes immortality.

Their walls were painted with scenes from daily life as if it were a home where everything suggested life. New possibilities arose during the Middle Kingdom. The dead could remain by their mummies, or they could enter the realm of the dead, called the duat, ruled by the god Osiris. The dead whose mummies were well preserved were free to move about on the earth and in the other world. Those whose mummies had been destroyed were happy in the world of the duat.

During the New Kingdom, the *Books of the Dead* appeared. These contained the names and titles of the deceased, written on papyrus. They were rolled up, sealed, and placed with the mummy. These, perhaps the oldest illustrated books in history, were to guide the dead in eternal life. They also stressed the importance of personal responsibility on earth. According to these texts, the earthly actions of the deceased was evaluated by the goddess Maat. If the verdict of Osiris and the council of the gods was positive, the deceased was declared immortal.

Humans and Destiny

The Egyptians believed that human life was in the hands of the gods. But humans were responsible for maintaining the balance of the universe and the existence of life. The Egyptians also believed that creation and life were the work of a god who looked after his creation like a shepherd. The Egyptians believed that with prayer, believers would discover inner justice, moral order, and a sense of sin and repentance.

Scenes inspired by the Book of the Dead are pictured on these two pages. *Top, across the two pages:* The deceased is seen in the solar boat with the god Horus. *This page, top strip:* The deceased is being judged by Horus, Osiris, and the council of the gods. *Lower strip:* The deceased is led by the hand by the god Anubis to the weighing ceremony. Anubis performs the weighing, placing a little box, symbolizing the heart of the deceased and of his actions, onto one plate of the scale. On the other plate is a feather, symbol of Maat, goddess of justice. Under the scale there is a monster ready to devour all evil souls. The scribe god Thoth is recording the result. The soul, recognized to be just, is led into the other world, known as duat.

SHEPHERDS, BLACKSMITHS AND MERCHANTS

The imperial civilization of Egypt was unique. In the rest of Africa life went on according to traditions that had developed in the various regions and were related to the differing environments. There were specialized hunters in the southern regions, hunter-shepherds of the Saharan type in the northern and eastern regions, and isolated farmers and vegetable growers in the west and in Ethiopia.

The African Iron Age

Between 1000 B.C. and A.D. 1000, Africa entered an Iron Age. This period was marked by the following four basic features: the spread of iron technology, the expansion of Bantu blacksmith-shepherds, the development of towns outside the Nile region, and the creation of travel routes within the continent and across the Indian Ocean.

In Africa the Stone Age and Iron Age overlapped. The technique of iron smelting appeared on the north African coast after 1200 B.C. Many scholars believe that this knowledge spread from the Mediterranean coast along a western route connected to Carthage and along an eastern route from Egypt to Meroe between the fifth and fourth centuries B.C. But recent discoveries have proved that iron had already been used in Nigeria in the eighth century.

The Early Nok Civilization

Around 1000 B.C., the valley of the Niger River became a gathering point for newly developed trade caravans that carried salt and perhaps slaves through the Sahara Desert. This activity, combined with a crop-growing and stock-raising tradition and the introduction of iron, increased population in some tribal centres. These centres became the first towns outside Egypt and the Mediterranean regions: first, Djenne (about 300 B.C.), and later, towns of the Nok culture in Nigeria.

The Nok society was rural, with merchants, blacksmiths, and artisans. Its towns were organized into enlarged family groups. The head of a town was a king who had authority over all its families. Each family group was made up of three or four generations living in several circular huts. The Nok towns also had special temples in honour of their ancestors and tribal heroes. In the early centuries B.C., these towns became the most active markets of West Africa.

The Bantu: Blacksmiths and Shepherds

In the same period, blacksmith workshops appeared around Lake Chad. They rapidly spread throughout the Congo Basin and also appeared in eastern Africa (Tanzania, Zambia). These sub-Saharan blacksmiths used unique methods of metalworking. Their methods, which produced a kind of steel, were not related to the methods used in Meroe or in Aksum where huge quantities of iron objects were manufactured using northern techniques. On the contrary, sub-Saharan methods showed the influence of Bantu people. The Bantu people were shepherds and growers who had spread into the Congo Basin from Nok. From there, small groups of these people, who already used iron, scattered throughout the equatorial-tropical areas at the centre of Africa, as far as Zambia. The Bantu people's superior technology probably allowed them to dominate the native Paleolithic populations.

East Africa

The only countries where the Bantu tribes did not penetrate were Ethiopia and Kenya in eastern Africa. There, an economy based on cattle, sheep, and goat raising had developed between 2000 and 1000 B.C. These regions were inhabited by people of the Kushite language group. Eastern Africa remained in many ways a cultural island, more directly connected to Asia than to Africa. Starting about 1000 B.C., eastern Africa became part of an important sea route that connected Africa to Indonesia along the northern arc of the Indian Ocean. Through this route, oriental jewellery, pottery, plants, and animals were introduced to Africa.

This sculpture depicts a human figure in a position of devotion. It is perhaps connected with ancestor-worship.

A hermaphrodite deity is given both male and female physical features. This sculpture comes from Djenne, Mali.

A human face made of terra-cotta was found at Djenne. Its features are very similar to those of the peoples living in the region today.

African kingdoms south of the Sahara during the centuries before and after the birth of Christ are shown on the map. The first towns, in the middle and low Niger valley, and the spread of iron and of the Bantu populations are part of the movement of civilization during this time. The territories of Carthage, of the African Greek colonies, of Egypt, and of Rome are not marked.

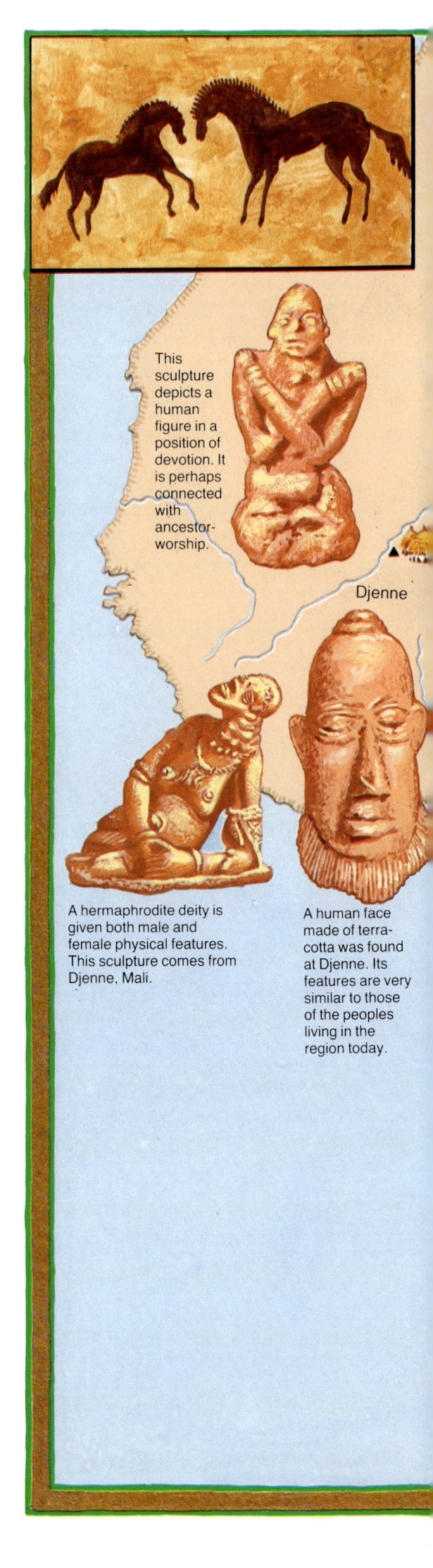

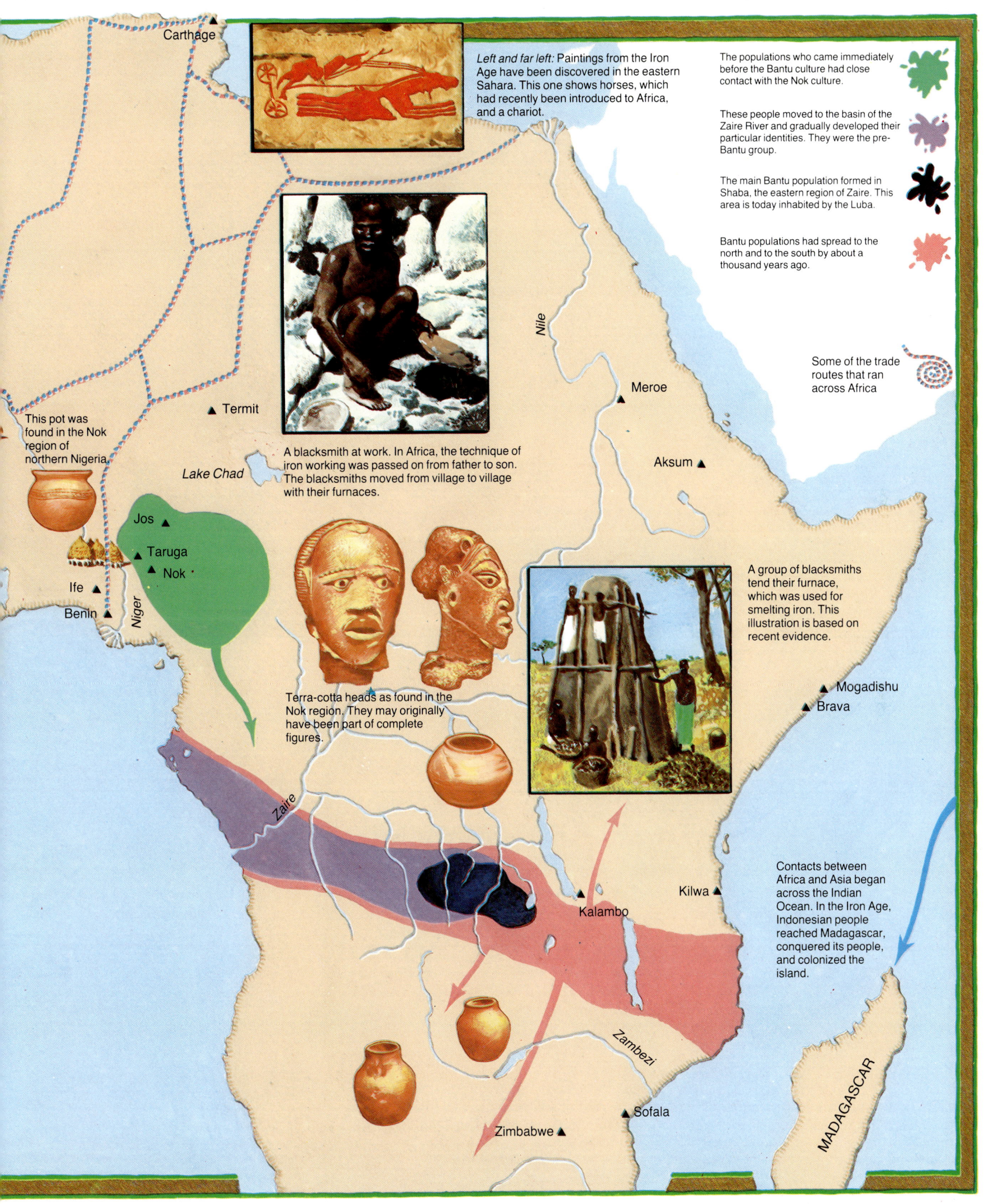

Left and far left: Paintings from the Iron Age have been discovered in the eastern Sahara. This one shows horses, which had recently been introduced to Africa, and a chariot.

The populations who came immediately before the Bantu culture had close contact with the Nok culture.

These people moved to the basin of the Zaire River and gradually developed their particular identities. They were the pre-Bantu group.

The main Bantu population formed in Shaba, the eastern region of Zaire. This area is today inhabited by the Luba.

Bantu populations had spread to the north and to the south by about a thousand years ago.

Some of the trade routes that ran across Africa

This pot was found in the Nok region of northern Nigeria.

A blacksmith at work. In Africa, the technique of iron working was passed on from father to son. The blacksmiths moved from village to village with their furnaces.

Terra-cotta heads as found in the Nok region. They may originally have been part of complete figures.

A group of blacksmiths tend their furnace, which was used for smelting iron. This illustration is based on recent evidence.

Contacts between Africa and Asia began across the Indian Ocean. In the Iron Age, Indonesian people reached Madagascar, conquered its people, and colonized the island.

Carthage was founded as a commercial settlement. *Insert:* The city was a customary stopping point along the sea route from Phoenicia to Spain.

CARTHAGE: ITS BIRTH AND DEVELOPMENT

According to tradition, Carthage was founded in 814 B.C. by Phoenician colonizers coming from Tyre. At that time, some Phoenician settlements already existed along the African coast, but they were small sites meant to serve as trading posts for the exchange of goods with the populations inland. The position of Carthage on the Mediterranean Sea, however, favoured its development over other Phoenician towns.

The Phoenician colonists settled in a region inhabited by Berber peoples. These were livestock-raisers and primitive growers, living in simple social groups based on family clans. The Phoenician colonists, more powerful as a result of their military and commercial organization, took power and turned Carthage into a major city-state. Gradually, Carthage became independent from its mother country and developed the Punic civilization.

The city was equipped with two harbours: a rectangular one for commercial ships and a circular one for warships. Not far from the rectangular harbour was the tofet, a sacred area for sacrifices. The higher part of the city was built on the hill of the Byrsa, an inner fortress surrounded by high walls. Another outer wall protected the entire city. The houses were built three or four storeys high, and the city streets were narrow. The harbour area, with its large dock, warehouses, and market place, was one of the most active centres in the Mediterranean Sea. Through this activity, Carthage became a great political

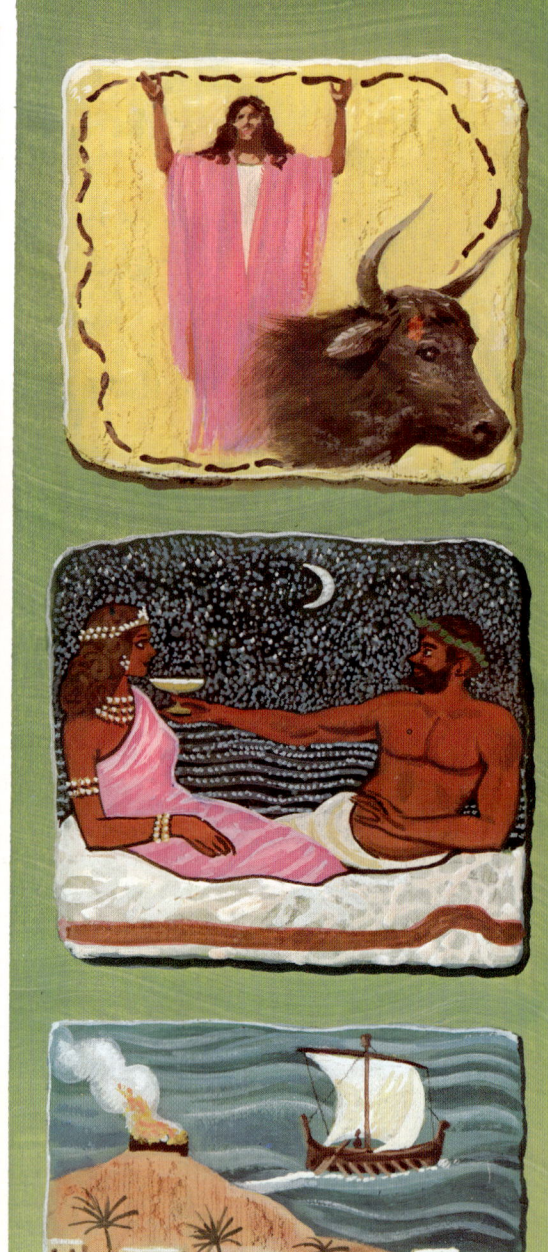

The Legend of Dido

The legend of the foundation of Carthage is based on the story of Dido (also called Elissa), daughter of King Belus of Tyre. Dido fled to Africa from Tyre after her brother, Pygmalion, killed her husband, Sychaeus. There, King Jarbas offered her a piece of land as large as could be contained inside an ox skin. Dido cut the ox skin into thin strips and managed to encircle a large territory with it. There she founded Carthage. Later, King Jarbas asked Dido to marry him, threatening to destroy Carthage if she did not agree. Dido, in order not to betray the memory of her husband Sychaeus, killed herself. The legend was picked up by the Roman writer, Virgil, who in the *Aeneid* described the arrival of the Trojan hero, Aeneas, in Carthage. According to Virgil's story, love blossomed between Aeneas and Dido. When Aeneas left Carthage, Dido killed herself.

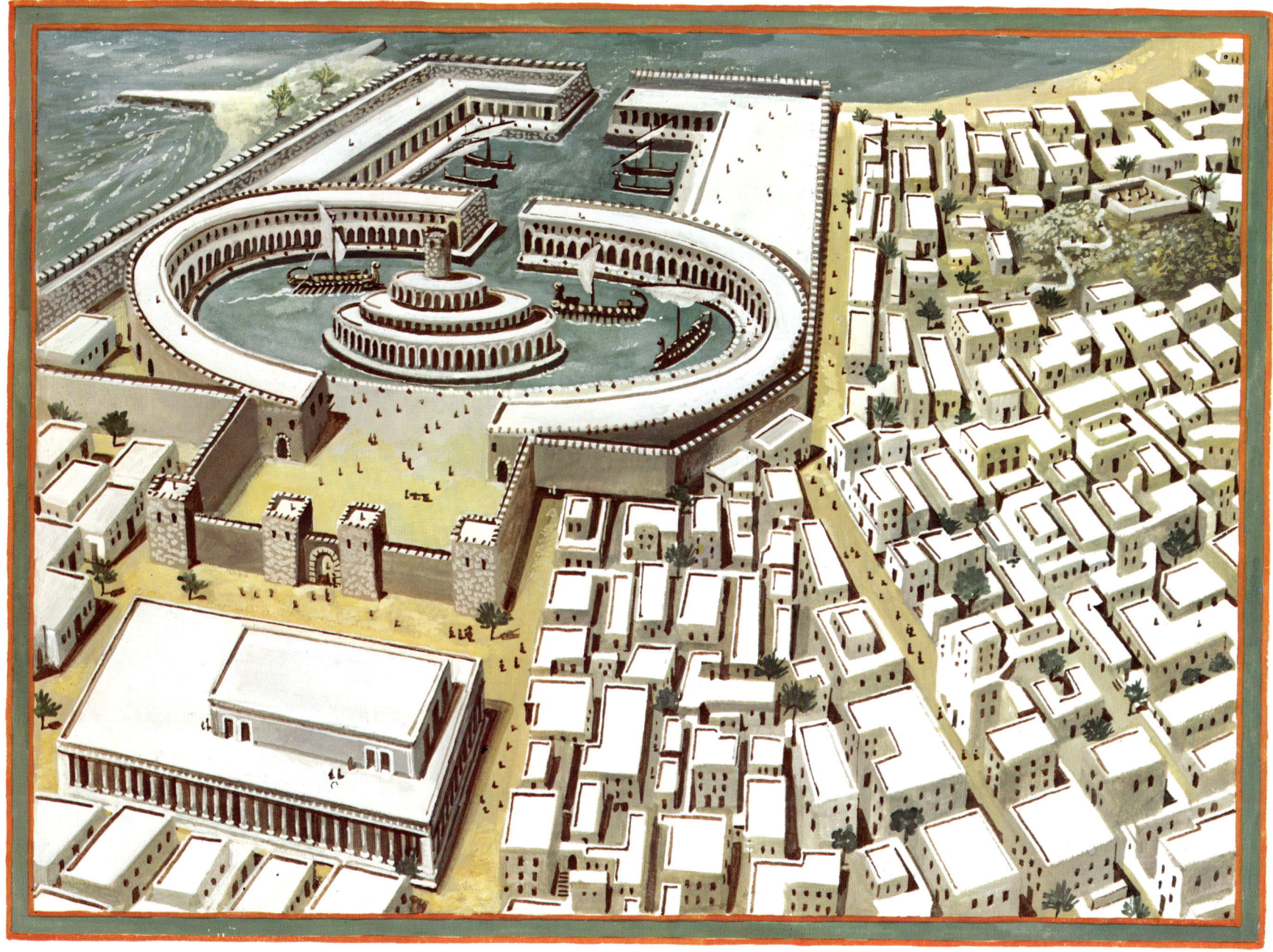

Carthage as it was at the peak of its development, seen from the top of the fortress. Ships can be seen in the twin harbours beyond.

Right: Diagram to show the government structure of Punic society.

and economic influence in the western Mediterranean regions. Within a short time, these regions became an almost exclusive trade territory for the people of Carthage.

The Government

The government of Carthage was an oligarchy. In this type of government, a small group of people rules. In Carthage, power was held by several wealthy merchant families. From this group, two suffetes, or judges, were elected each year. The suffetes had the executive and judiciary powers. The Small Council, which was also part of the government, had thirty members elected for life. This council held legislative power, along with the Large Council, which had three hundred members. The latter gathered only on special occasions when the suffetes and the Small Council could not reach an agreement on an issue. The Assembly of the People had various powers related to public life.

The army, which was separate from the political power, was made up mainly of hired foreign soldiers, or mercenaries. Punic citizens held most of the higher military ranks, and formed the majority of the navy.

The Religion

The Punic religion was based, for the most part, on the Phoenician religion. Punic deities, such as the goddess Tanit, the god Baal Hammon, and even the god Melquart who was "king of the city," were of Phoenician origin. Rituals consisted mainly of sacrifices to the gods, performed to summon their protection or to give thanks for help received. The priests, who performed the rituals, sacrificed animals and even children inside the tofet.

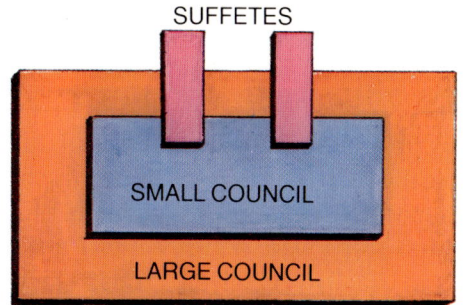

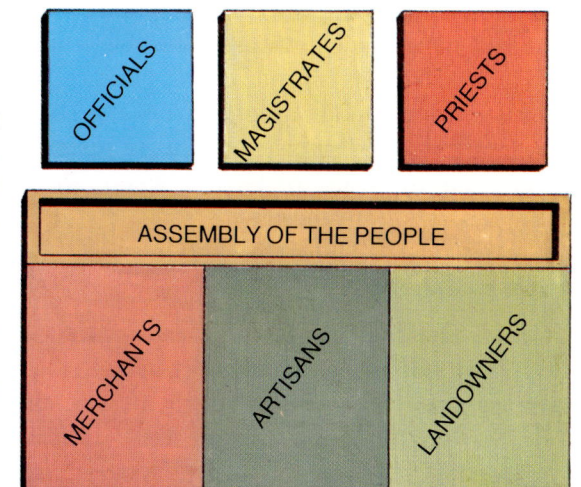

CARTHAGE: ART AND TRADE

Commercial and Political Control

As mentioned earlier, Carthage was built in an extremely favourable strategic location, protected both on the sea and towards the land. Its position also made the city central to Sardinia, Italy, the Balearic Islands, southern Spain, and Corsica. Much of this Mediterranean territory would eventually come under Carthaginian control.

In the seventh century B.C., Carthage became independent. To secure itself, Carthage formed alliances with foreign powers such as the Etruscans in Italy. Alliances were necessary to face the Greek city-states that were also a force in the Mediterranean area. In 540 B.C., the Etruscans and the Carthaginians drove the Phoenicians from Corsica and cut into Greek territory in southern Spain. This was an important step toward control, and Carthage expanded its power by establishing colonies throughout the Mediterranean area.

Recent archaeological excavations have revealed that the so-called colonies were not merely points of trade. On the contrary, they were highly organized settlements with military control and power over the area's conquered populations, who were heavily taxed and burdened with obligations. In short, Carthage had an extended political dominion and a commercial empire. Only the Carthaginians dared to sail beyond the Straits of Gibraltar. They could sail to the British Isles in search of tin or travel to Africa to trade for gold and ivory.

Cargo Ships and Warships

The Carthaginians perfected the structure of the so-called Mediterranean ship, which became a model for all the fleets of ancient times. The cargo ships were sturdily built, massive, wide, and usually propelled by sails. The ships of war were fast and easy to manoeuvre. They depended chiefly on rowers for power, but used sails when the wind was favourable.

Re-exporting was an interesting practice in Carthage. Many goods brought from the East were not used in Carthage, but were instead re-exported to Spain or Sicily, where they could be traded for other goods.

The Harbours

Due to the great emphasis placed on trade, the city's harbours were highly organized. The island which lay opposite to them was an excellent lookout point for the city. But it blocked the view of the harbours to ships coming from the open sea. The dockyards, which were surrounded by a double wall with gates, were almost invisible from the outside.

Art and Culture

The people of Carthage have often been depicted as being concerned only with profit and not interested in art. It is difficult to draw such conclusions, since the local culture of Carthage was almost completely destroyed by Romans after 202 B.C.. But it is obvious that other cultures influenced Punic culture and art. The strong influence of the Greek spirit mingled with the eastern ways which the Carthaginians brought with them from Phoenicia. Greek language and customs were widely used by the upper classes, and Hannibal, the great Carthaginian leader, even wrote military strategy in Greek. The Carthaginian constitution itself was drawn up by direct comparison with the constitution of Greek towns. In spite of all this, Phoenician language and writing maintained an eastern nature. These traders produced literature that was read throughout the classical world. Some historical, geographical, and scientific writings were of great importance.

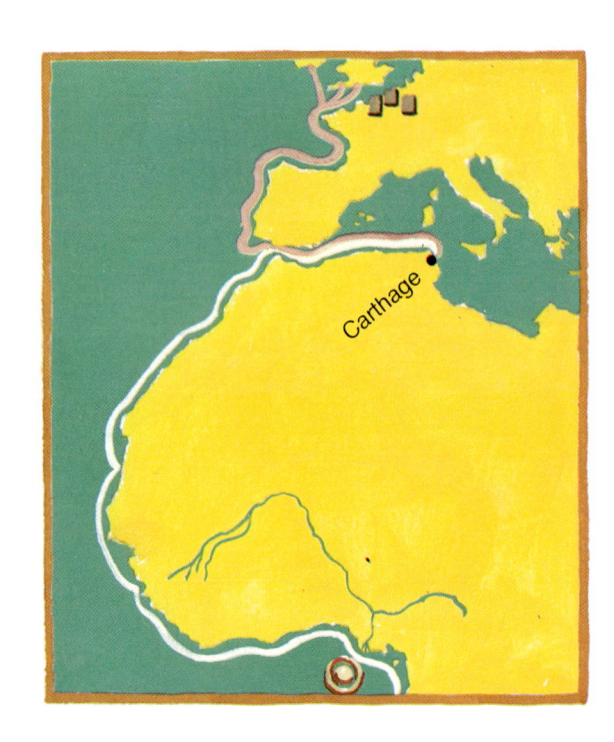

Journeys and explorations are recorded on this map. The pink line indicates the Atlantic tin route. The white line shows the route followed by Hanno, the Carthaginian geographer who explored the African coast.

The spread of the Carthaginian Empire in the Mediterranean region is shown on this map. Pink lines indicate the main commercial routes.

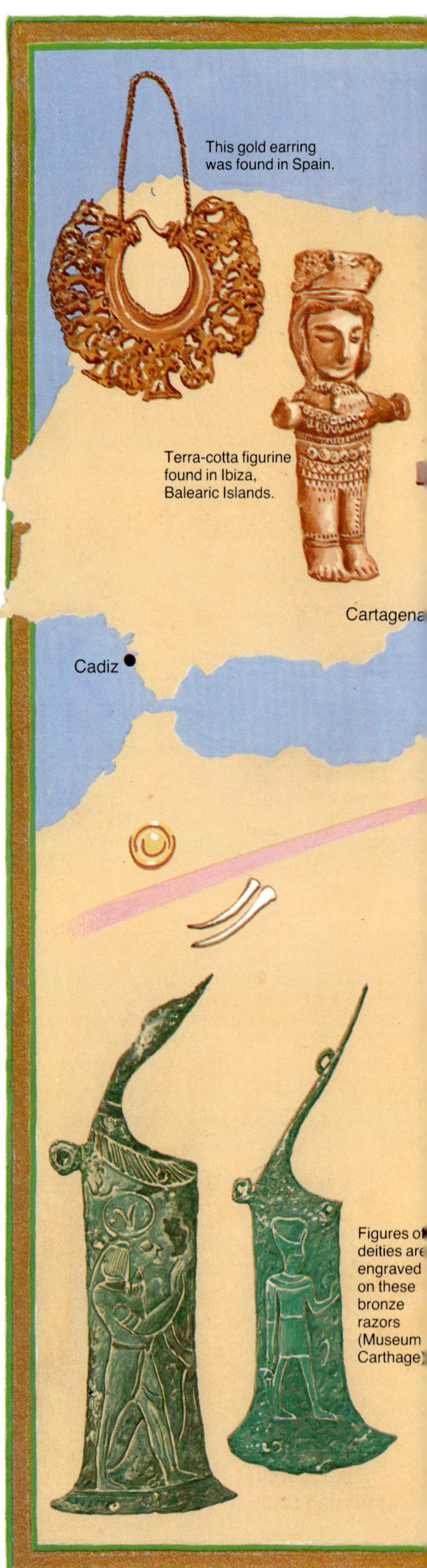

This gold earring was found in Spain.

Terra-cotta figurine found in Ibiza, Balearic Islands.

Cartagena

Cadiz

Figures of deities are engraved on these bronze razors (Museum Carthage)

Female figure, found in Barcelona, and carved from alabaster. She holds a container in her arms and sits on a throne flanked by sphinxes.

A religious artifact from Bitia, Sardinia.

Small ivory carving of a head found in Sardinia.

	Silver
	Tin
	Ivory
	Gold
	Wheat
	Wine
	Oil
	Ceramics

Marseille

Rome

Olbia

Head-shaped necklace pendant made of glass from Cagliari (Sardinia).

Taranto

Ibiza

A terra-cotta female figure from Ibiza.

Cagliari

Mozia

Syracuse

A female head showing Greek influence, from Sicily.

CARTHAGE

A terra-cotta Carthaginian mask.

Stele, discovered in Mozia, Sicily.

Two Carthaginian ships reconstructed from remains which were found near Marsala, Sicily.

Stele grave marker, with images of its owner and of Hercules, found in Tunis.

Green jasper scarab from Sardinia showing two figures of Egyptian influence.

A feminine face (left) showing Greek influence and a male figure with curly hair and a beard (right), now in the Barcelona Museum.

47

THE KINGDOM OF KUSH

The southern part of the Nile Valley, south of Egypt, was called Kush in ancient times. Here, between the sixth century B.C. and the third century A.D., a kingdom developed that had great political power and was of major importance in the spread of new techniques and ideas throughout Africa.

What is known of the Kush kingdom comes from archaeological work and information from ancient writers such as the Greek historian Herodotus, the Greek geographer Strabo, and the Latin scholars Seneca and Pliny. However, direct written sources are absent. Only a few examples of the Kush language remain today, carved in the stones of sacred buildings. Hieroglyphic and cursive writing were used, both derived from Egyptian writing. They have not as yet been decoded. Around 1500 B.C., Egyptians invaded the Kush region. The conquerors introduced their system of government to the local populations of farmers and semi-nomadic shepherds. Around 750 B.C., the region freed itself from Egyptian control, which had become very weak. One of the Kush kings, Piankhy, invaded the Nile regions and started a period of Kush domination over Egypt that lasted until 654 B.C.

The Kush kingdom's first capital was the town of Napata on the Nile, where sculptures of the first kings have been found. Around the beginning of the sixth century B.C., the town of Meroe began to gain importance. Meroe was located to the south in a fertile area suited for agriculture and livestock-raising, and rich in iron-bearing minerals. The site was also favourable for trade.

Religion and Art

The Kush culture was influenced by that of Egypt in many ways. In particular, the Kush religion adopted many Egyptian deities and rituals, although it also had original gods, such as the lion-god Apedemek.

Egypt's influence was also evident in the shape and decoration of both artwork and objects of daily use, such as vases and jewellery, especially during the first centuries of the Kush kingdom. From the third century B.C. on, original artistic elements emerged, principally in clay work. Terra-cotta objects were decorated with small human or animal figures, while metal objects showed features derived from Near Eastern and Mediterranean cultures.

Agriculture and Livestock-Keeping

The Kush kingdom's economy was based on agriculture, livestock-keeping, and trade. The cultivation of grain, especially millet, was widespread along the Nile and in the southern area of the region around Meroe. In fact, this territory was richer in water resources than the northern parts of the country.

The problem of irrigation was solved with two simple devices that were used to draw water from wells and rivers. The first device was the shaduf, which is a pole with a bucket at one end. The second device was called a saqia. It was a large wooden wheel used to draw water from wells and was powered by an ox. Livestock-raising was characterized by the

Meroitic writing, inscribed on a clay tile. The central scene depicts Anubis and a goddess.

The carved lid of a bronze mirror shows a deity on a lotus flower.

The lid of this clay vessel depicts a struggle between a lion and a man.

This gold earring was part of a funeral collection.

A gypsum statue, part of a funeral collection.

Gold earring set with a semi-precious lapis lazuli stone.

dominant presence of cattle. Cattle breeding was made possible by the relative abundance of water in the area. Goats, sheep, donkeys, and elephants were also domesticated.

Trade and Trade Routes

The kingdom was located at the meeting point of several trade routes. To the north, the Nile connected Kush with Egypt and with the Mediterranean region. An eastern land route ran all the way to the Red Sea, and from there sea routes led to Arabia, Persia, and India. From the west came the caravan routes, which connected the region to the rest of Africa.

Due to the Kush kingdom's favourable location, many valuable African goods passed through its territories on their way to the Mediterranean and Near Eastern markets. These goods included ivory, leopard skins, ostrich feathers, ebony, and gold, as well as goods from beyond the Indian Ocean to be traded in the west.

A Kush king rides an elephant. These animals were used by the army.

Kush men: the drawings are based on a Persian bas-relief found at Persepolis.

MEDITERRANEAN SEA

Memphis

The Kush Empire was located in the southern part of the Nile valley. Its first capital was Napata, and its later capital was Meroe. The arrows indicate the trade and caravan routes leading to Egypt, the Sahara region, equatorial Africa, and the Red Sea.

The "saqia" was an ingenious wheel device used to irrigate the fields with water from a river.

Thebes

RED SEA

The expedition of the Kush king Piankhy, who conquered Egypt and ruled it for a brief time.

A village of bottle-shaped huts. Cattle, sheep, and goats were reared.

Nile

Napata

The "shaduf" was used to draw water from the Nile to irrigate the fields.

Meroe

Fortresses were built along the caravan routes.

49

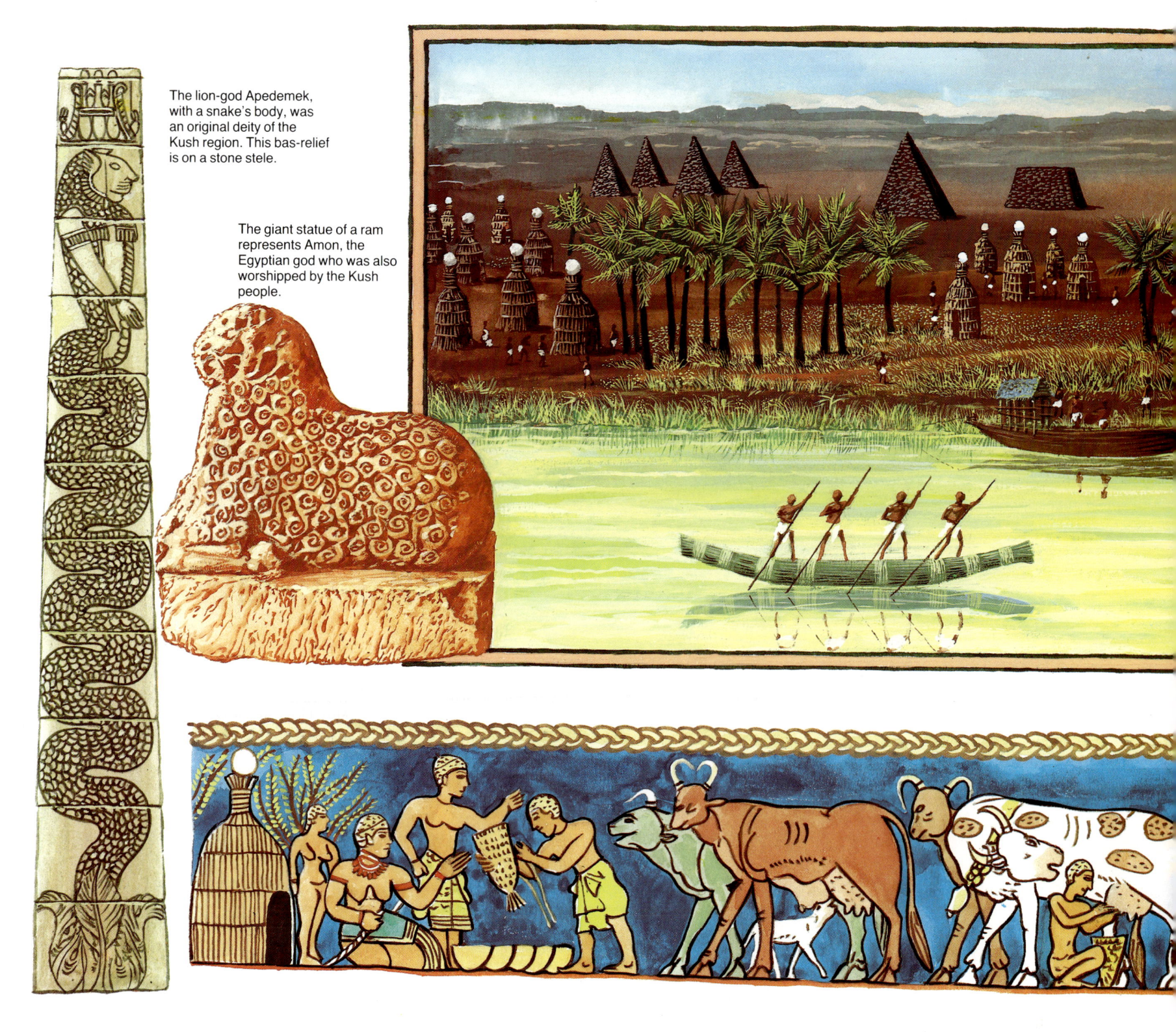

The lion-god Apedemek, with a snake's body, was an original deity of the Kush region. This bas-relief is on a stone stele.

The giant statue of a ram represents Amon, the Egyptian god who was also worshipped by the Kush people.

MEROE, CAPITAL OF THE KUSH KINGDOM

A Magnificent City

The city of Meroe was at its greatest splendour between the third century B.C. and the third century A.D. In this period it was the capital of the Kush kingdom and the residence of the king and of the royal family. From the third century B.C., the city also became the seat of royal burials.

The city stretched over a broad, flat area bordered by the Nile to the west and by a succession of low hills to the east. In ancient times, Meroe was known as a splendid city. It had imposing buildings made of brick and stone, such as the complex of the royal residence with the baths, the temple of the Sun, the temple of the lion-god Apedemek, and the impressive stretches of pyramids of the royal cemetery. The people of the city lived in simple houses made of sun-dried brick or in huts, and many people maintained their semi-nomadic lives as shepherds. They would settle near the river during the dry season and move to other areas during the wet season.

Kings and Queens

The Kush kingdom had a monarchy similar to that of Egypt. However, it had some original features, such as its order of succession to the throne. In Kush, when a king died, the throne was not taken by his son, following a direct father-to-son descent. Instead, the king's brother took the throne. This method emphasized the lineage of the mother. In fact, the king's mother was an important figure in the court. She was considered a queen and was given the name of "Candace." Early historians sometimes mistook this title for a first name. The priests also had great authority within the state structure. In some cases, the priests even

The city of Meroe, seen from the Nile River. In the background are the pyramid-shaped royal tombs.

The scene above depicts the iron-smelting for which Meroe was famous.

Farmers honour the queen. This illustration is based on a decoration on a bronze cup from Karanog.

had the power to dismiss the king.

The Iron Industry

The great wealth and economic importance of Meroe resulted from an iron industry that began in the first century B.C. The area was rich in iron ore, as well as in the wood that was necessary to fuel the furnaces. These resources encouraged the production of iron tools and weapons, which were then traded, especially in other African territories. It is probable that Meroe helped spread the use of iron throughout central and western Africa.

The Decline of Kush

In 23 B.C., a Roman expedition headed by Publius Petronius invaded the northern part of the kingdom. However, the invasion did not result in military occupation. The Kush government maintained its independence as well as its political and economic relationships with Rome. In fact, the Latin culture influenced the development of Kush art.

The bathhouse attached to the royal palace of Meroe and other buildings in which local and classical architectural elements are combined date back to this period.

The Roman occupation of Egypt, however, had negative effects on the Kush kingdom's trade, and the economy declined in the second and third centuries A.D. Royal burials are much smaller and less opulent than those of earlier times. Also, Kush control over the territory had grown weak. Around A.D. 350, the army of the Aksum Empire defeated that of Meroe, marking the end of the Kush kingdom. Three Christian kingdoms, called Nobatia, Makuria, and Alodia, arose in the region from the sixth century A.D. The area acquired its modern name of Nubia.

THE KINGDOM OF AKSUM

The territory once held by the Aksum Empire lies on a plateau near the southern end of the Red Sea. This plateau is separated from the Red Sea by a strip of land, part of which is below sea level. This area was among the most inaccessible in the ancient world. Yet here a civilization with southern Arabic characteristics developed five centuries before the birth of Christ. This new civilization, called Aksum, (which means "the land which is green with grasses") developed in the territory of present-day Ethiopia.

The kingdom of Aksum became important in the first century A.D. and reached the peak of its power around the third century A.D. By that time, it had conquered many smaller kingdoms. Its control extended from Ethiopia to upper Nubia, and from southern Arabia to the fourth cataract of the Nile.

Palaces and Houses

Aksum's kings were known for their impressive buildings. Aksum royalty often lived in large, magnificently decorated palaces. The tendency toward pomp and grandeur was also expressed in the large public buildings. Many of these were built of large square stones that stood off the ground on foundations. An interesting custom was the use of wood, stones, and mud together as building materials. The major buildings in Aksum were Enda Michael, Enda Simon, and Takija Mariam. The Takija Mariam was known as the largest palace of eastern Africa and was probably the royal residence.

The typical houses of Aksum were square with four rooms, or niches, at the four corners. The rooms were connected by corridors that ran along the outer walls. The walls were built of basalt and sandstone blocks, cemented together with mud. Windows were few and small. Round huts were also common.

The Obelisks

Aksum was the city of the great obelisks. Obelisks are huge, usually four-sided, stone pillars. At least one hundred of them remain today. Some of them are rough blocks of stone 7 to 8 metres long. Others have square or rectangular sections, are finely carved, and are embellished with decorations.

The Stone Thrones and Colossal Statues

The stone thrones were another impressive feature of the Aksum civilization. Cosmas Indicopleustes, the traveller and geographer from Alexandria, mentioned a magnificent throne dedicated to Ares. It was carved from a solid piece of white marble and decorated with splendid images of gods. Some thrones were royal seats; others were used by the imperial judges. Thirteen of them were placed in front of the cathedral of Aksum.

Cosmas Indicopleustes also wrote of the great stone carving skills of the Aksum people. He mentioned a colossal statue about 100 metres from the Takija Mariam, one of the city's major buildings. Only the base of this statue remains today. Some Sculptures of animals have also been preserved, but there are no examples of paintings.

Part of a limestone frieze from Adulis.

A design set in marble found at Adulis.

Map showing the kingdom of Aksum and its main towns.

The obelisk of Aksum still stands today.

Right: The city of Aksum at its peak (around the first century A.D.). The city was located on a plateau, and its roads were often built like flights of steps carved into the rock. In the foreground stands a small temple with a "royal throne" covered by a thatched roof. Temples of this type were common. Numerous obelisks were erected in the city. They had religious purposes and were decorated with carvings depicting various aspects of religion, politics, and the king's life. The people lived in thatched huts like those shown here. Beyond them, in the background, is the royal palace of Takija Mariam. This was the most important of the numerous palaces in the city.

The people of Aksum used a combination of timber and stones in the construction of their buildings.

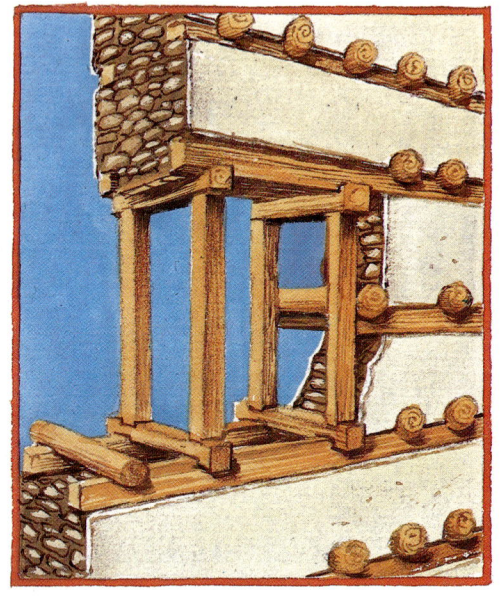

A partial view of the palace of Enda Michael.

53

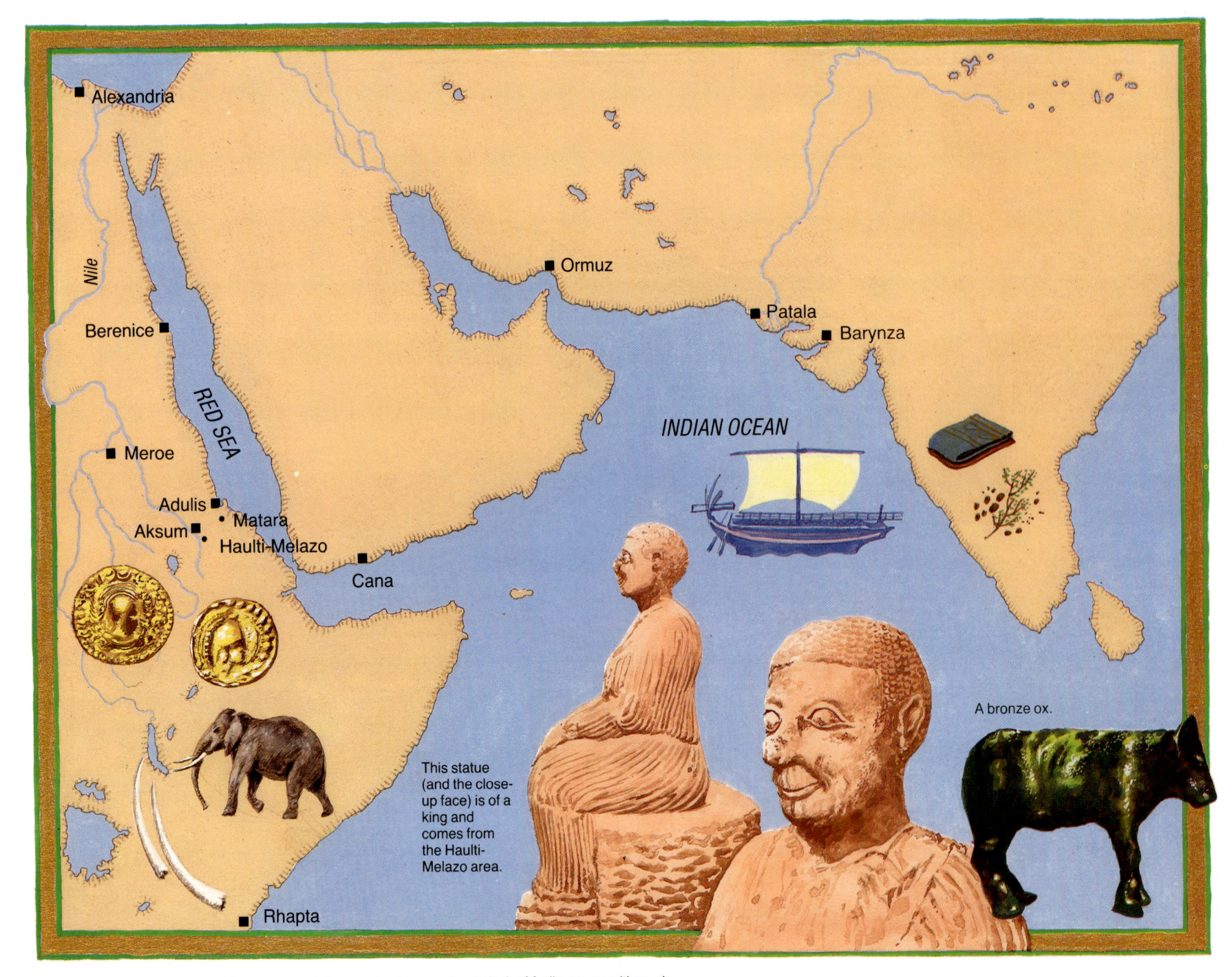

This map shows the commercial expansion of the people of Aksum towards the Mediterranean (through Egypt) and towards India (across the Indian Ocean). Among the traded goods were precious metals, elephants, fabrics, spices, turtle shells, ivory, and incense.

AKSUM: TRADE, RELIGION, CULTURE

The Harbour Town of Adulis

The towns of Melazo and Matara were founded by the people of Aksum around the fifth century B.C. Aksum, which was to become the capital of the empire, was founded about fifty years later. The harbour town of Adulis, which is said to have been founded by a group of runaway slaves, developed near today's town of Massawa in the third century B.C.

As a port, Adulis was the starting point for ships that carried gold, incense, the much-prized Ethiopian elephants, and ivory to Asia (India in particular) and to the Mediterranean. Because of this activity, the town grew quickly and became wealthy. Ivory was especially important to the Romans, and they obtained most of it through Aksum. When Meroe began to decline, the shrewd people of Aksum also took over the iron trade. They imported glass from Arabia, olive oil from Italy, grain and fabric from Egypt, sugar cane, rice, and sesame oil from India, and wool from Arsinoe.

Since trade was constantly growing, the kingdom of Aksum began to produce coins a few decades after the foundation of Adulis. This made Aksum the first state of eastern Africa to have its own currency. The coins were mainly bronze and bore likenesses of the kingdom's great kings, such as Endybis, Aphilas, Caleb, and Ezana.

Agriculture and Livestock-Rearing

Farming activities in Aksum consisted mainly of the production of staple crops. Grape growing was also important. The land in dry areas was skilfully terraced and irrigated. Livestock-rearing was also practised, and cattle and sheep were the principal animals kept by farmers.

The Religion

When the people of southern Arabia moved to Africa, they brought with them their religious traditions and their deities. The religion was centred on the sacred triad: the

The rolling hills that stretched inland from the Red Sea were a fertile area, partially cultivated with vineyards and partially used for rearing livestock. On the coast, the Aksum people built the town of Adulis. Adulis soon became the main port for commerce between the Red Sea and the Indian Ocean.

The Aksum kingdom was the first state of eastern Africa to produce coins. Here are the two faces of a coin found in Meroe.

Ethiopian writing was very important for all of eastern Africa. Pictured here are the beginnings of the great inscription of King Ezana.

god Moon, the goddess Sun, and the Morning Star. Naturally, names of gods and cults changed with the different settlements. The introduction of the goddess of the earth, Meder, marked a change in the nature of the earlier, star-centred triad. A series of lesser gods ('Am, Gad, and others) and of spirits of the waters, seas, and trees accompanied the main gods. The cult of the vulture and that of the snake were widespread, and superstitions were numerous.

After almost eight centuries of polytheism (worship of many gods), the Aksum civilization was introduced to Christianity. According to some sources, Christianity first began to spread in some of the commercial Greek-Egyptian colonies located near Adulis. Native groups probably became followers of the Christian faith even before it was officially accepted in the royal court. In any case, the work of Frumentius was important to the spread of Christianity. He had been sent by Saint Athanasius, the Patriarch of Alexandria, and around 330 B.C., he converted King Ezana to the Christian religion. King Ezana eventually made Christianity the official religion of Aksum.

Aksum Writing

As the Aksum Empire developed, it eventually took on characteristics of its own, which in turn became the traditions of present-day Ethiopia. Aksum's language, which was that of the southern Arabian people, was soon replaced by the Ge'ez language. This ancient language is considered the first truly Ethiopian language. The writing of the Arabian people, however, was maintained in Aksum for a long time. The first clearly Ethiopian writing, in fact, dates back to the second century B.C.

Ships carrying roots of the silphium plant to various countries sailed from the harbour of Cyrene. Even the king was present during the weighing of the valuable cargo. This illustration is based upon the decoration of a Greek cup, called the cup of Arcesilaus.

The cup of Arcesilaus II shows the weighing of silphium, 560 B.C.

This silver coin comes from Cyrene 425 B.C. The image on it represents the nymph Cyrene with the silphium plant.

THE GREEK COLONIES IN LIBYA AND IN EGYPT

Colonies on the Coast of Libya

Early in the eighth century B.C., the populations of the Greek towns on the Aegean Sea began to expand and eventually reached Africa. In 631 B.C., Greeks founded the town of Cyrene on the Libyan coast. Soon, other towns were founded, both along the coast and inland. In Libya, the Greeks found fertile soil for farming. The area soon became famous as a nursery for the rare plant silphium. This plant's roots were used as medicine and food. In Cyrene, the Greeks also developed important trade activities, mainly involving wheat, wool, and ox skins.

As the Greeks pushed into Libya, they sometimes met with resistance from the native people. But soon the two peoples set up a commercial relationship. The Greeks treated the Libyans as a free population, and eventually the two groups mixed through marriage.

Saitic Egypt and Greece

During this time, Egypt was feeling the effect of a growing Assyrian Empire, which occupied territory along the Tigris River. In 671 B.C., the Assyrians pushed their way into Egypt and took power. The invaders, however, could not control all of Egypt themselves and entrusted some power to certain loyal delta princes. One of these princes, Psamtik of the town of Sais, used this opportunity to seize total control. Naming himself king, he united the northern part of Egypt and began a new dynasty known as the Saite dynasty.

The Saite pharaohs restored the traditions of the past and worked to unite the kingdom further. One of the pharaohs, Necho, started the digging of the Channel of the Two Seas,

To the left and below: Two vases from Miletus were found at Naucratis.

A Greek ship and in cross section its load of amphoras – large, oval storage jars.

The map shows Greek colonization in Egypt (*red arrows*) and in Libya (*green arrows*), as well as the route of the expedition of Pericles (*blue arrows*).

Plan showing part of the town of Naucratis, with the great sacred buildings in the centre.

Below: The region of Abu Simbel is shown with a detail of the colossal figures that were erected in front of the temple. These are among the largest rock-carved figures in the world. *Bottom:* This graffiti inscription is the signature left on the colossus of Abu Simbel by a Greek mercenary who served in the Egyptian army.

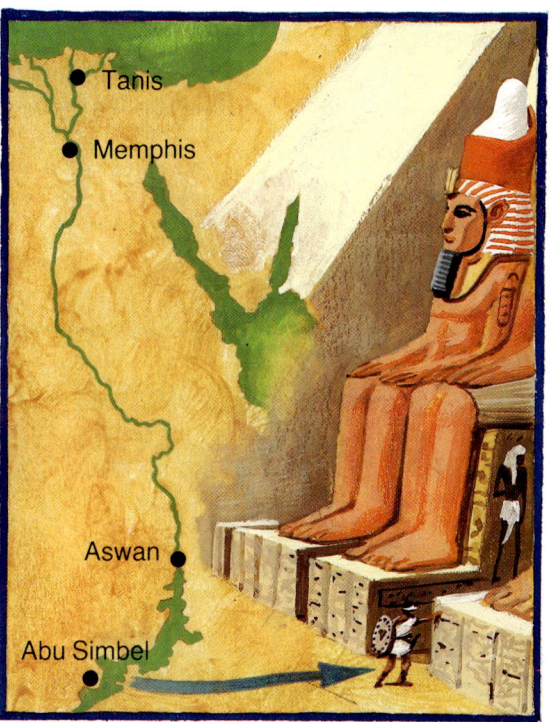

which was to connect the Mediterranean Sea with the Red Sea. (Not until the 19th century was this project actually carried out, with the excavation of the Suez Canal.) Necho also worked on developing Egyptian trade. This led to contact between Egyptians and Greeks.

Only one Greek colony, Naucratis, was founded in Egypt, around 620 B.C. It was located on a Nile outlet and was founded by Greeks coming from various towns. By the will of the pharaoh, all trade with Greece was concentrated in this town. Naucratis soon became a centre for wheat trade in the Mediterranean. A large Greek population lived in the colony, and a communal sanctuary, called Hellenion, was built to remind all the colonists of their common Greek origin. The relationship between this Greek town and the neighbouring towns was not always smooth. In fact, the Egyptians rebelled several times against the Greeks.

In spite of their differences, the relationship between the Greeks and Egyptians grew stronger during three centuries of contact. It grew especially strong when Greek trade was no longer limited to Naucratis but could spread to all the Egyptian trade towns. The Greeks were fascinated by the great age of Egyptian culture and religion. The Greek historian and geographer Herodotus travelled to Egypt around 440 B.C. and wrote a fascinating account of Egyptian society.

As ties between Egypt and Greece grew, many Greeks migrated to Egypt. Overcrowding in Greece encouraged this trend. Many Greek mercenaries (hired soldiers) even fought in the Egyptian army. In fact, Greek mercenaries were the most reliable soldiers in periods of internal conflict in Egypt.

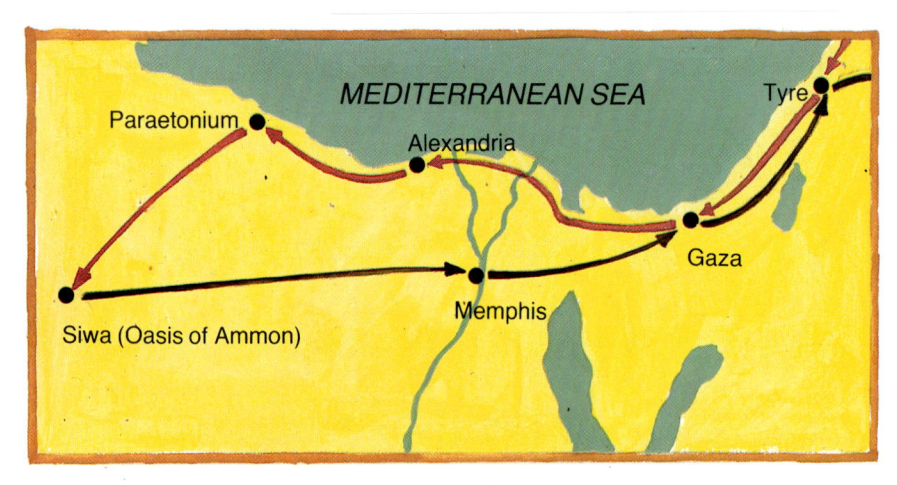

The route of Alexander the Great to the Oasis of Siwa.

The location of Alexandria: To the north was the Mediterranean Sea, with a small island that sheltered the coast from the open sea. To the south was a broad inland lagoon. When Alexander reached this place, only the small village of Rachotis existed.

Alexander and his soldiers reach the oasis of Ammon. The sanctuary at the oasis was famous in the Greek world because of its oracle, to which people came to ask questions of the god Ammon.

THE GREEKS CONQUER EGYPT

The Expedition of Alexander the Great

In 353 B.C., the Greeks were invaded by Philip II, king of Macedonia. After he had defeated the Greeks, Philip turned toward Persia, intending to conquer this great empire. But he was killed in 336 B.C. before he could complete his plan. Philip's son, Alexander the Great, carried it out instead. In 334 B.C., he marched into Persia and defeated the Persians on the banks of the Granicus River. A year later, he defeated Darius III, king of Persia, in the Battle of Issus. These victories opened the entire Persian Empire to Alexander.

Before moving towards the heart of the empire, in Asia, however, Alexander descended on Egypt. At the time, Egypt was under Persian rule, as it had been since the Persian king Cambyses defeated the Egyptians. During his conquest, Alexander did not meet with resistance from the Egyptians, who had come to hate the Persians. Moreover, he was backed by the many Greeks who lived in Egypt at the time.

In Egypt, Alexander founded a new city along the coast. This city, built in the Greek style, was named Alexandria. Many factors encouraged the rise and development of the new city. A small island off the coast sheltered the shore, forming a well-protected harbour. Moreover, Alexandria was located on the Nile Delta and was close to a large inland lagoon that furnished excellent waterways leading inland. At that time, commerce between the Mediterranean, the Red Sea, and the Indian Ocean was developing rapidly. Alexandria soon became a very active centre of commerce.

The Visit to the Oasis of Siwa

Still on the march, Alexander and his army continued along the coast. In Libya, they turned south and advanced across the Libyan

A reconstruction of the plan for the oasis of Ammon shows the three circles of walls.

The priests used small boats like this to obtain the oracle's response. The illustration is based on descriptions given by Greek historians.

The Oracle of Ammon at Siwa

Throughout the Mediterranean world there were major religious centres, such as the oasis of Siwa. In these centres, various gods were honoured, and in some cases it was possible to consult an oracle. This was a way of communicating directly with the god, obtaining knowledge of his will and answers to various questions. The centres were not connected to only one group of people. People from different countries would visit the sites on a pilgrimage. Thus, these were major meeting points, where peaceful relationships developed.

The Roman historian Curtius Rufus gave the following description of the oracle of Ammon in Siwa: "What is honoured as a god does not have the form which the artists usually attach to gods. It looks very much like a disc and is formed by an emerald and various precious stones. When a response is asked of it, the priests carry it inside a sort of gilded boat.... Matrons and girls follow it, singing a simple song in their native language ... to induce [the god] to give a clear response."

Left: An image of Alexander inscribed on the face of a coin.

desert to the oasis of Siwa. The oasis, which was surrounded by desert, was green, filled with cultivated olive and palm trees. Siwa was the most important centre of the cult of the god Ammon. Ammon was originally the Egyptian god Amon-Re, whose cult was also widespread among the Libyan tribes to the west. The Libyan Greeks had come to know Ammon and identified him with the principal god of the Greek pantheon, Zeus. In their towns, the Greeks venerated the god Zeus-Ammon, who was symbolized by a man with ram horns. From Cyrenaica, the cult of Zeus-Ammon had spread to all of the Greek world. The temple of Siwa was famous mainly because it hosted the oracle of the god.

A major event occurred as Alexander neared the temple. The oldest of the temple priests proclaimed him the son of Zeus-Ammon. This meant that Alexander was the ruler of Egypt because in the Egyptian tradition the son of Amon-Re is Horus, the pharaoh. Having been declared a direct offspring of Zeus, Alexander also held a special position among Greek people. At the temple, Alexander was also told that he would rule the world.

Alexander, Pharaoh of Egypt

Alexander had great admiration for the Egyptian civilization. Because of this, he understood that Egypt could only be ruled by a pharaoh. Alexander, as a result of the oracle's proclamation, was considered divine and he was crowned pharaoh during his return journey from Siwa. This title assured him the loyalty of Egypt and Cyrenaica during his military campaign in Asia.

EGYPT DURING THE HELLENISTIC PERIOD

The Government of the Ptolemies

When Alexander died in 323 B.C. in Babylon, his generals split his vast empire among themselves. The Macedonian general Ptolemy I took over the government of Egypt. Proclaiming himself king, Ptolemy I began the dynasty known as the Ptolemies. The kingdom thus created was one of the many states resulting from the division of Alexander's empire. These states were commonly referred to as "Hellenistic monarchies." The term *Hellenistic* refers to the period following the death of Alexander the Great in which Greek culture flourished.

The new king chose Alexandria as his new rulers, it became an important centre of Greek culture. A museum, known as the Temple of the Muses, and its library were founded here by Ptolemy I. The collection of manuscripts held here included the most important cultural texts of the time. Many famous scholars and writers came to Alexandria, where they formed a literary school. These writers produced a great deal of original work and are responsible for preserving earlier Greek writings such as Homer's work and the Greek tragedies.

The Greek population of Alexandria was also very skilled in scientific and technical achievements. They were concerned with astronomy, medicine, and geometry. Among

Thus, the relationship between Egypt and the Mediterranean world was complex. Foreign rulers maintained relationships with local priests and took part in their synods (councils). Some cults were celebrated by both, since various Greek gods were identified with Egyptian gods. Religious decrees were even written in three languages: Greek, spoken Egyptian, and religious Egyptian (hieroglyphics). Some Greeks could speak Egyptian, and many Egyptians knew Greek. However, in the last two centuries B.C. Egyptian rebellions were a threat to Alexandria's rulers and weakened their power.

Much rivalry continued between the Ptolemies and the other Hellenistic rulers. The

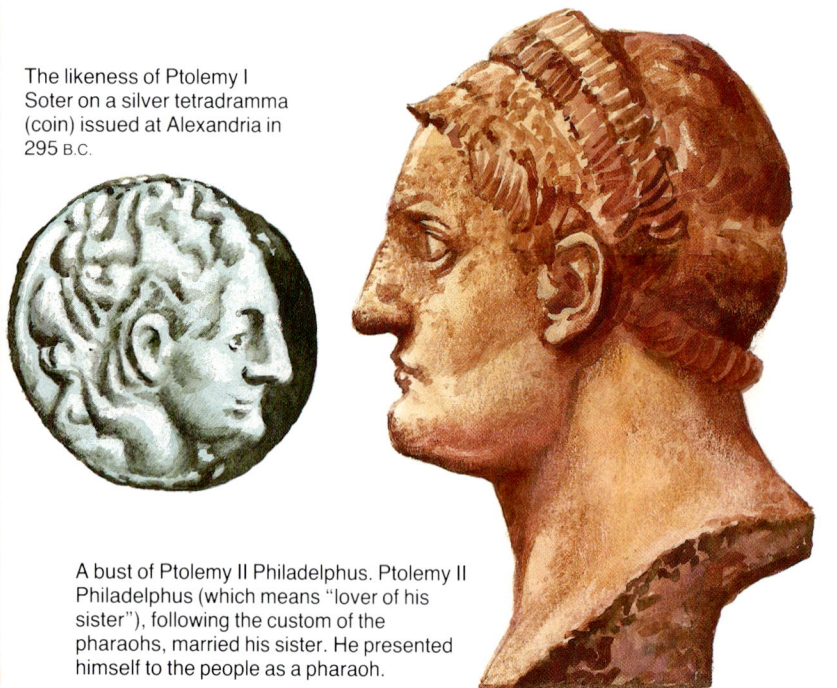

The map shows the expansion of the Ptolemaic kingdom under Ptolemy III. Alexandria was where most of the Greek population of Egypt lived.

The likeness of Ptolemy I Soter on a silver tetradramma (coin) issued at Alexandria in 295 B.C.

A bust of Ptolemy II Philadelphus. Ptolemy II Philadelphus (which means "lover of his sister"), following the custom of the pharaohs, married his sister. He presented himself to the people as a pharaoh.

The face of Arsinoe II, wife of Ptolemy II Philadelphus.

capital. Within a few generations, this city became the most important harbour of the eastern Mediterranean. A large lighthouse (Pharos) built on the little island across the harbour became the city's symbol, and it was known as one of the Seven Wonders of the World.

Alexandria, a Major Cultural Centre

Alexandria was a bustling city with a mixed population of traders, officials, Greek soldiers, and merchants from various Mediterranean countries. Its wealth came from trade. In many ways, the city was similar to many other Greek cities scattered throughout the Mediterranean. But through the work of the most famous scholars were Euclid, a physicist and mathematician; Eratosthenes, who calculated the earth's diameter with great accuracy; and Archimedes, a mathematician and inventor.

Greeks and Egyptians in Ptolemaic Egypt

Egypt's identity at this time came from the overlap of the Egyptian and Greek cultures. Greek culture was dominant, but aspects of Egyptian culture were also present. Farmers continued their traditional growing patterns that were connected to the cycles of the Nile. Artisans and priests kept Egyptian religion alive. Ancient centres of Egyptian culture were also still active, especially in the south.

Ptolemies fought a total of six wars against the Seleucids, the sovereigns of Syria, trying to get possession of the Celesyria region (Lebanon). The territory of Egypt reached its maximum expansion in the reign of Ptolemy III (247-221 B.C.). Later, the Ptolemies were forced to retreat under pressure from the Seleucids.

Opposite page, top insert, right section: The interior of an ancient library. All libraries of ancient times used the famous library of Alexandria as their model.
Top insert, left section: The process of papyrus-making and a finished papyrus roll are shown.

The main picture shows the harbour of Alexandria with its famous lighthouse.

61

Far left: The route followed by Atilius Regulus and battle sites from the first Punic War. *Left:* Atilius Regulus in front of the senate of Carthage.

The diagram *far left* shows the battle of Zama, which ended the second Punic War. The cavalry wings of the Roman army, in red, encircled the Carthaginian army after chasing away the enemy cavalry. *Near left* are Hannibal and Scipio Africanus.

Scipio Aemilianus weeps over the ruins of Carthage, which he did not want to destroy.

Incidents from the three Punic Wars.

THE ROMANS CONQUER AFRICA

The Punic Wars

Carthage had become the capital of a vast empire on the western coast of Africa. By the third century B.C., this empire stretched all the way to the Straits of Gibraltar. At the same time, Rome was a growing power within the Mediterranean region. As both groups struggled for power, tension rose and finally burst into open fighting.

The result was the Punic Wars. These three wars, all of which Carthage lost, took place between 264-146 B.C.. The first conflict broke out when Rome fought Carthage's attempt to control the Strait of Messina between Sicily and Italy. To protect its territories, Rome increased its naval power to rival that of the Carthaginians. With a fleet of battleships, the Romans, under their commander Atilius Regulus, won an important sea battle in 256 B.C. at Cape Ecnomus. Several other important victories gave Rome command of the sea by 241 B.C., the year in which the first war ended. After this, Rome gained control over Sicily and Sardinia. At the same time, the Carthaginians conquered Roman territory in Spain, making up for the islands they had lost.

The Second Punic War (218-201 B.C.) was caused by territorial rivalry in Spain. This war made famous the great Carthaginian military leader Hannibal. Hannibal led the army right into Italy, conquering vast territories and threatening Rome. The Romans reacted with a successful plan, devised mainly by the general Scipio Africanus. They kept the Carthaginians in Italy, isolating them from the rest of their empire. Meanwhile, other Roman troops regained Spain in 206 B.C., separating Hannibal from a source of supplies and troops. This move was followed by an attack on Carthaginian home territories. When Scipio landed on the African coast in 204 B.C., he was met by Carthaginian troops and their Numidian allies under King Syphax. The Numidians were a tribe of Africans formerly ruled by King Masinissa. Masinissa, who had been over-

The Berber mausoleum at Medracen was the centre of a Numidian city.

A Roman coin depicts Jugurtha, the subjugated king of Numidia, kneeling in front of the Roman general Sulla.

A merchant ship sails from Africa bound for Rome. It is carrying ivory and wheat.

The above writing is an example of writing in the Numidian alphabet. It is read from right to left.

A Greek-Phoenician funerary monument, where local aristocrats were buried. (Thugga, 100-200 B.C.)

The progressive conquest of northern Africa by Rome.

thrown by Syphax, allied himself with the Romans and regained his kingdom at the end of the Second Punic War. A battle at Zama in 202 B.C. signalled this end and a complete victory for the Romans.

In the following years, Carthage re-emerged as a threat to Rome. Many Romans favoured the destruction of Carthage. At the end of the Third Punic War, the Roman consul Scipio Aemilianus was forced to raze Carthage to the ground, although he was opposed to this destruction. A Roman province, called Africa, was established there in 146 B.C.

The Conquest of Numidia and Mauretania

After the Punic Wars, Numidia under Masinissa expanded west. Eventually, it stretched from the Roman province to Mauretania, whose territory bordered the Atlantic Ocean. Upon Masinissa's death, Numidia was divided into three kingdoms. They were organized around several towns that served as trade centres. This area was very important for wheat cultivation.

After the defeat of Carthage, many Romans wished to expand into this African area. When Roman settlers were killed in the city of Cirta, many Romans saw this as an excuse to start a war. But at this time, Numidia had once again united under the king Jugurtha. So the war, begun in 111 B.C., was not easy for Rome. Finally, the Roman general Gaius Marius ended it by capturing Jugurtha in 105 B.C. Rome put a new ruler on Numidia's throne, and a wave of Roman colonization began.

In 46 B.C., Numidia became involved in a Roman power struggle between Pompey and Julius Caesar. The Numidian king, Juba, sided with Pompey and was defeated by Caesar. This battle marked the end of Numidia, which became part of a new Roman province in what is today Algeria. Thus, Rome was no longer merely protecting its interests or creating military outposts. It was involved in conquest and colonization.

The kingdom of Mauretania, however, maintained its identity for a while even under Roman control. Finally, the last king, Ptolemy, was called to Rome in A.D. 40 and was sentenced to death for unknown reasons. In 42, two new Roman provinces were created, called Mauretania Caesarensis and Mauretania Tingitana.

Cleopatra

Below: In the battle of Actium, in 30 B.C., the fleet of Octavian (*in red*) defeated that of Antony and Cleopatra (*in black*).

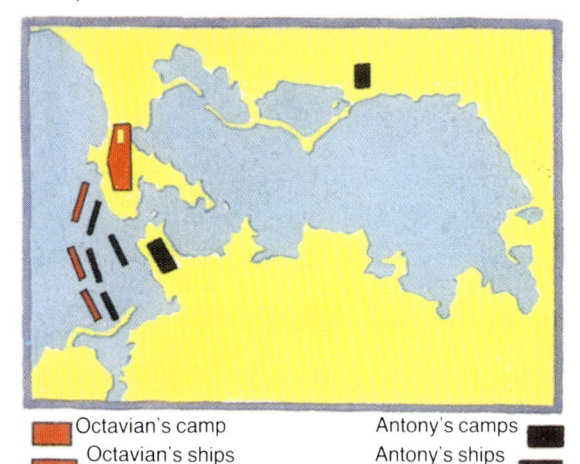

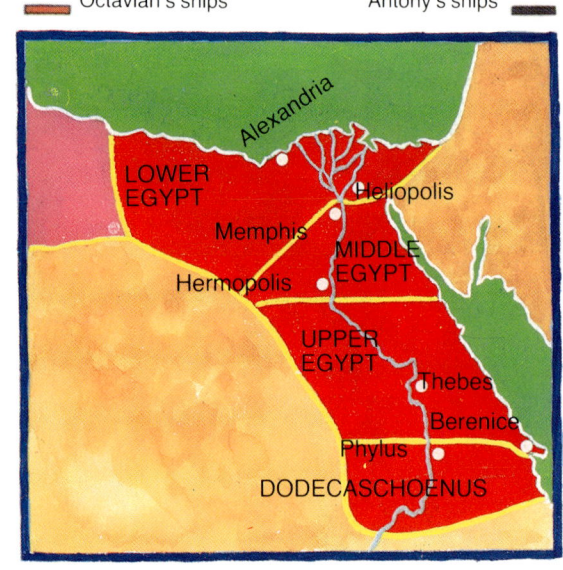

- Octavian's camp
- Octavian's ships
- Antony's camps
- Antony's ships

This map shows the administrative subdivision of Egypt under Roman rule.

This drawing of a procession in honour of the goddess Isis is inspired by the description given by Apuleius in his "Metamorphoses." *Insert above:* A Roman ship arrives on Egyptian shores. *Insert below:* Farmers plough their field with oxen.

EGYPT UNDER ROME

The Conquest of Egypt

In the first century B.C., struggles for power in Rome were resolved in Egypt. After Caesar's death, his heir, Octavian, and two other military leaders, Mark Antony and Marcus Lepidus, formed a triumvirate (a three-person alliance). Lepidus was soon pushed aside, and Octavian and Mark Antony battled for control. Antony, seeking Egypt's aid in this struggle, married Egypt's queen, Cleopatra, in 36 B.C. In 31 B.C., Octavian's fleet defeated that of Antony and Cleopatra in the Battle of Actium. A few months later, the Romans conquered Alexandria, and Antony and Cleopatra committed suicide.

Egypt Becomes a Roman Province

After 30 B.C., Egypt became a Roman province. However, the country's religious and cultural tradition, and its economic and military importance, led the conquerors to rule Egypt in a special way. The Romans partially reorganized the economy and administration of the country. Alexandria ceased to have an independent administration. Egypt had to pay a yearly tribute of wheat to Rome, and a special organization was created to maintain this huge flow of goods.

To obtain the wheat, Egypt had to collect great amounts from its farmers. As a result,

A statuette of Isis nursing a child symbolizes the deity from whom Egyptians believed humans drew strength and nourishment. The goddess Isis was worshipped at the time of the pharaohs. At the time of Roman domination of Egypt, Isis became one of the main deities.

many farmers fled their fields and sought shelter in the swamps of the Delta region. In spite of this, rebellions and disorders were rare, and the country was ruled in a peaceful way. Hard times for Egypt, as well as for the other African provinces, were yet to come. By the third century A.D., Berber people from Africa's Mediterranean coast began to raid the southern provinces, and the power of Rome's emperors weakened.

Like other invaders before them, the Roman rulers also presented themselves as heirs of the pharaohs. Egypt's ancient and therefore seemingly powerful religion was attractive to some emperors: Domitian favoured the Egyptian religion, while Trajan and Hadrian built monuments in the grand style of the pharaohs. Intellectual life remained lively throughout Egypt, and the priests practised religious rites in the ancient way.

The Cults of Serapis, Isis and Osiris

For centuries, Egypt had been part of the vast Roman Empire. Its presence greatly affected religion among the populations of the entire Mediterranean region. Since the Ptolemies, the cult of the god Serapis had been widespread. Serapis had been proclaimed the god of the kingdom, as he represented the blending of Greek and Egyptian religious elements. His name was similar to that of the ox-god, Apis, who was worshipped in Memphis. His image had a bearded face like that of Zeus. The cult of Serapis was also important in the Roman epoch.

The most important cult, however, was that of Isis and Osiris. Its influence was felt through out the Roman Empire. According to the Egyptian tradition, the god Osiris had been killed by his brother, who chopped him to pieces and threw him into the Nile. But Osiris's wife, Isis, put the pieces back together, and Osiris was brought back to life. Thus, the idea of resurrection was central to the cult. In Greek and Roman times, Isis, Osiris, and the event of Osiris's death and resurrection were celebrated in Egypt with grand processions through the streets.

The worship of Osiris also included special ceremonies, called mysteries, which only a few chosen followers attended. Those who took part in the mysteries received a promise of resurrection. Both in Greek and Roman religion, human life was ruled by destiny. This destiny could not be changed—even by the will of the gods. Through the mysteries of Osiris, people believed they were able to break free of this fatalistic creed.

ROMAN AFRICA

The Last Rebellions

Peace was not immediately achieved in Roman Africa. For decades, wars and rebellions shook the inner territories, especially those along the desert. Gradually, however, Roman influence penetrated the conquered territories. Towns then developed, partially on Numidian-Punic lines and partially with new foundations. Around five hundred towns existed in northern Africa at this time.

Economic Development

Land was an important source of wealth and social prestige. It was especially important as a source of wheat, which was used to pay the tribute to the conquerors. Cultivation was increased by the Roman practice of turning nomadic people into farmers and through the construction of large irrigation systems. Production was organized around farmhouses placed in the middle of a piece of land. The owner-administrator's house was surrounded by other buildings. These were used as slave quarters, animal stables, or storehouses. Commercial activities also flourished during this time. The harbours developed, fairs were held in the small inland villages, and market places were built in the towns.

Roman-African Society and Culture

Within two centuries, the thinking of many African peoples changed, creating a new world in which Roman and African cultures blended. The towns were the heart of this change. Each town, even the smallest, had a forum, a judiciary basilica, a bathhouse, a library, and several temples. Life-styles in these towns

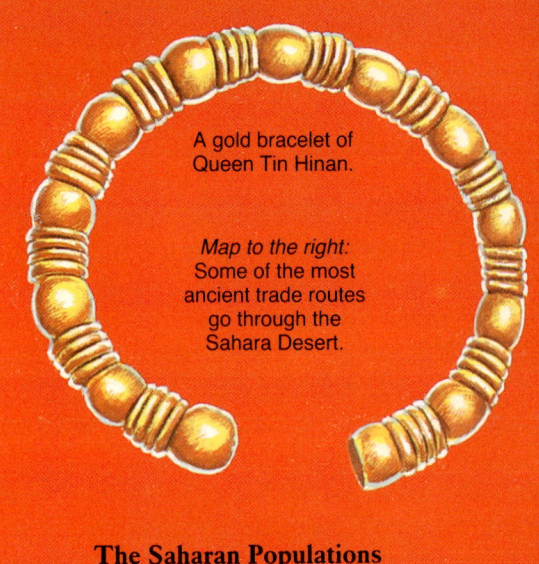

A gold bracelet of Queen Tin Hinan.

Map to the right: Some of the most ancient trade routes go through the Sahara Desert.

The Saharan Populations

The peoples living in the desert were forced by climate to lead a nomadic life and had only a few settlements. They were organized into tribes and spoke a language similar to that spoken along the coast. Around the first century B.C., they began writing. By this time, they had also developed trade routes. As a

North Africa during the Roman epoch, set in mosaic. The forts in red mark the line of the "limes," while the main towns are drawn in black. *The inserts show:* I) a villa, or farmhouse, inspired by a northern African mosaic; II) the arch of Septimius Severus in Lambaesis; III) Thamugadi, the gateway at the time of Septimius Severus; IV) the theatre of Sabratha in Libya. *In the oval inserts:* wine, wheat, and dates (all export goods). The animal figures are drawings based on mosaics from north Africa.

result, some of them became very wealthy and important. Roman objects have been found in desert tombs. These objects tell a great deal about the social importance of the dead. The tomb of Queen Tin Hinan in Abalessa, which dates back to the fourth century, contained gold and silver bracelets, and jewels.

were very similar to those in Rome. The wealth of the towns soon became the wealth of the upper class.

Africa's period of cultural growth took place in the second century A.D. The storyteller Apuleius, the jurist Salvius Julianus, and the orator Fronto lived at this time. Moreover, schools teaching the art of mosaics developed. The marvellous works of art from these schools are still preserved today. The African spirit found its highest form of expression in the mosaics.

Romans in the Sahara

The Romans settled in land near the Sahara. This area was visited by nomadic tribes who brought items of trade or raided the territory during their periodic migrations. To mark the territory of the empire, the Romans created a border or "limes." This border, which was guarded by military forts, was a way to control and sometimes completely block exchanges between the desert world and the Roman provinces.

Around the first century B.C., the camel became widespread throughout the Sahara. This animal was invaluable to the nomads because it was so well adapted to desert life. It could cross all kinds of terrain and go for long periods without water. The camel replaced the horse as the most important beast of burden and changed the pattern of movement through the Sahara. The frequent use of wells was no longer necessary, nor was the transportation of large quantities of hay (needed to feed horses).

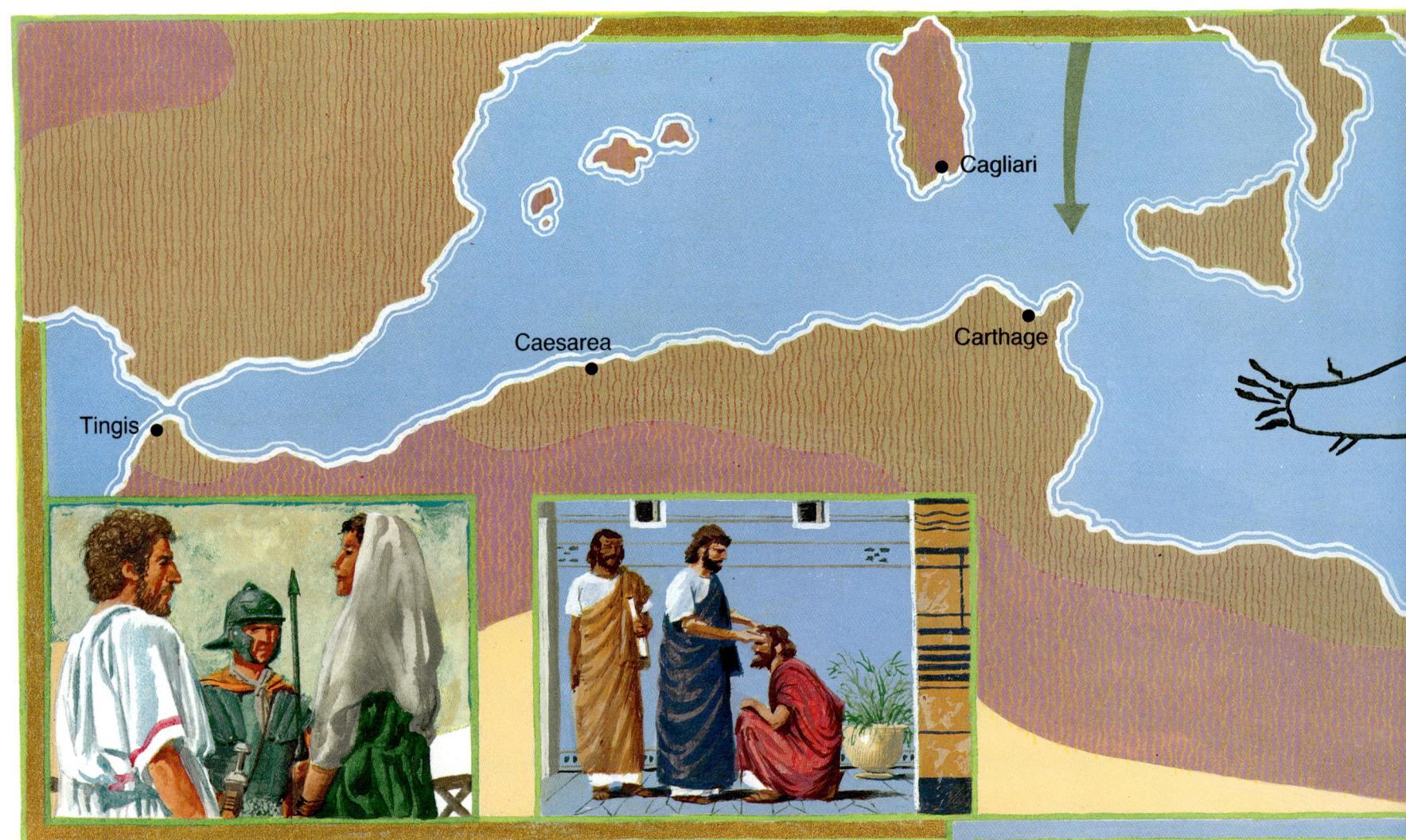

This map shows the Mediterranean Roman Empire and the spread of Christianity in north Africa at the beginning of the third century. *In the inserts, left:* Felicitas, one of the martyrs of Carthage in 203, goes to her trial. *Centre insert:* In Carthage, a Cyprian bishop pardons a Christian who had abandoned his faith during the persecutions. *Right insert:* A monastery, or cenoby, in the Egyptian desert and, *in the small insert*, a monk.

CHRISTIANITY

The Beginning of Christianity in Alexandria

According to tradition, Christianity was preached in Alexandria by the apostle Mark. The most ancient evidence of Christianity in Egypt is fragments of papyrus containing the Gospel of John, dating back to the second century. During this century, Christianity spread among the Hebrew and Greek populations of Alexandria, where in A.D. 190 there were already a bishop and some Christian scholars. In 202, the Emperor Septimius Severus threatened to punish anyone who converted to the Jewish or Christian religions. Some Christians were arrested and killed. Others were forced to flee. In spite of this, the Christian community of Alexandria continued to expand.

As a great cultural centre, Alexandria had many libraries and was home to many philosophers, poets, and scholars who strove to answer the questions about God and humanity that were widespread in the Hellenistic world. Some of these people were newly converted Christians. In Alexandria, they began the first theological school. There it was possible to study Greek and Hebrew sacred texts, as well as the new Christian religion.

The Birth of the Coptic Church

The church of Alexandria also became a missionary centre. Through it, the Gospel spread through Egypt and the neighbouring regions. The first missionaries spoke Greek; thus the first converts were Greek. Later, Egyptians who spoke Coptic, a language derived from Egyptian, accepted the religion. According to popular tradition, this was the birth of the Coptic church, still present in Egypt.

The Copts are also thought to have begun the monastic movement in the early church. This idea developed among the Egyptians and spread throughout the Roman province. The monastic life called for a person to live a solitary life in poverty and prayer. The followers, called monks, considered Roman life corrupt and Hellenistic culture sinful.

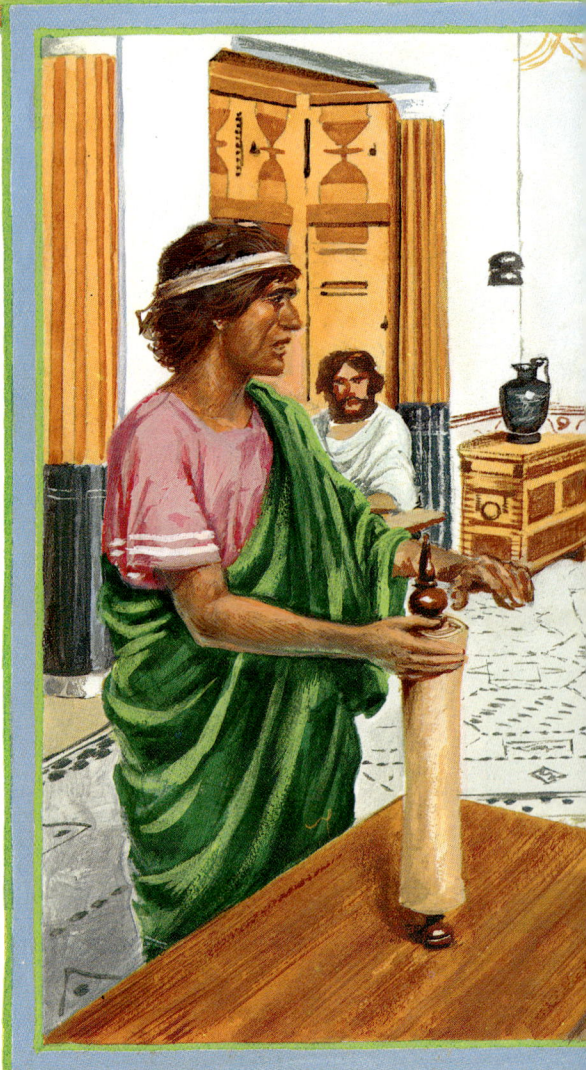

Left, below: In Alexandria, the theologian Origen explains the Christian faith to students.

Antonius, born around A.D. 250, was a major figure in the group of monks referred to as hermits, or anchorites. The anchorites lived an isolated life, weaving baskets and copying texts. They met each other only for weekly worship or on special occasions. Pachomius, who lived in the same period as Antonius, also lived in the desert. He chose a different way of life from that of the anchorites. He accepted the company of others because he thought that the individual grew best in a community. In this way, the first monasteries were created. The monks lived simply. They had to obey rules of behaviour, do manual work, attend worship, and pray. Instruction, common meals, and fasting on certain days were also required. Within a short time, monasteries spread throughout Egypt.

Christianity in Carthage and in the Western Provinces

The first missionaries to reach the Roman western provinces in Africa probably came from Rome. They spread Christianity among Hebrews and Romans. The capital of the province, Carthage, was a logical site for the spread of Christianity. In A.D. 203, the city's Christian population was already large, but it suffered severely from the persecutions of Septimius Severus.

In spite of this and other later persecutions, Christianity spread inland and to the west. It became very popular among the urban Romanized population. The most ancient Christian cemeteries in this area date back to the middle of the century. Soon, mosaics with Christian representations started to appear.

Two figures were prominent in this period: Tertullian and Cyprian. Tertullian, an excellent Latin writer, defended the cause of Christianity with passion and enthusiasm. He showed the pagans that Christians had every right to their beliefs. Cyprian was the bishop who guided the church of Carthage during the persecutions. He had a keen sense of the bishop's importance within the local church. He taught the importance of belonging to the church and of being able to declare oneself a Christian. He decided that Christians who, during the persecution had denied their faith, could be pardoned and again accepted in the church. Cyprian died in the persecution of Valerian in 258. Peace for the church in Egypt and in Africa, as well as all over the empire, came during the reign of Constantine, the first Roman emperor to become a Christian.

THE ANIMALS OF AFRICA IN PREHISTORIC ROCK-ART

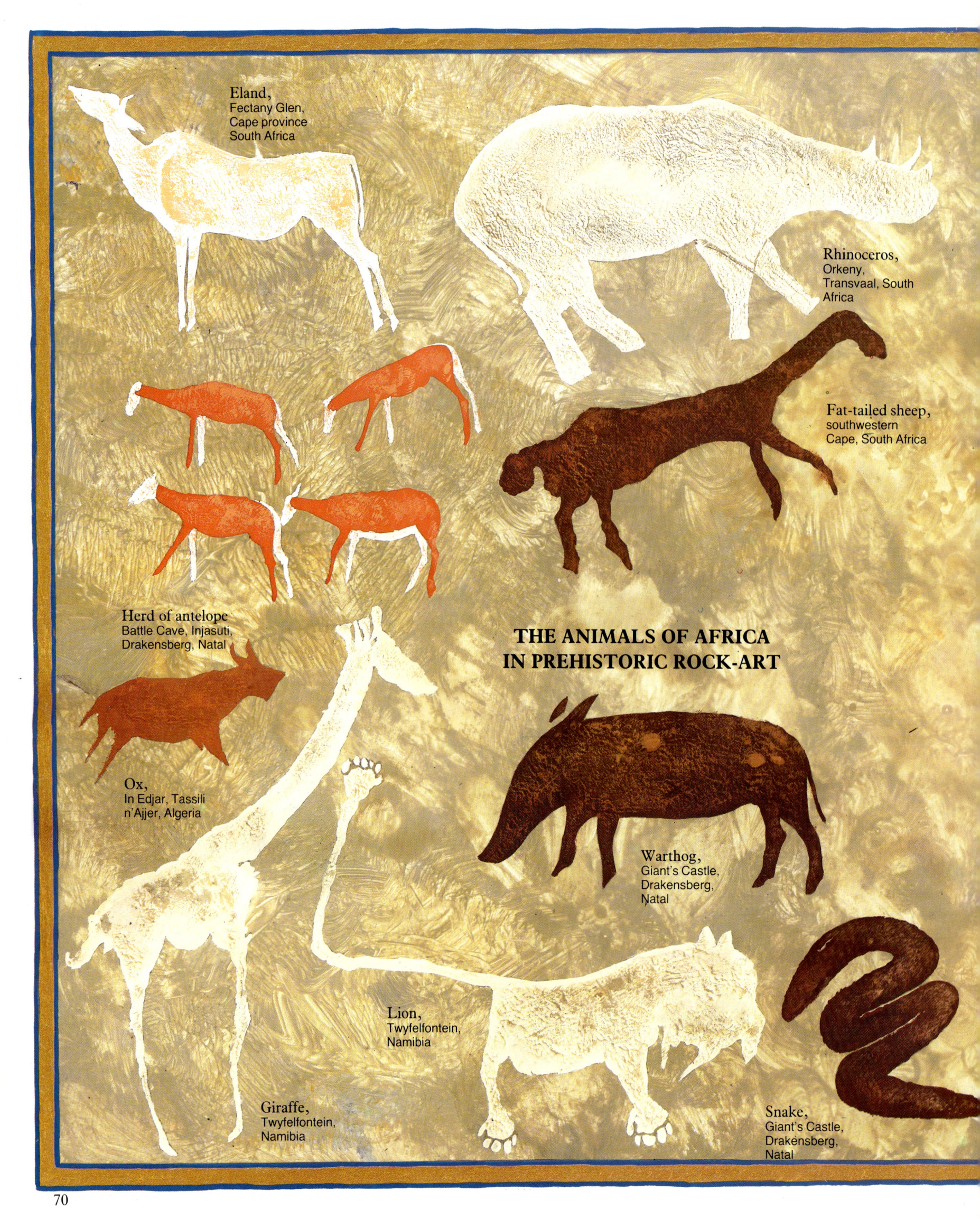

Eland, Fectany Glen, Cape province South Africa

Rhinoceros, Orkeny, Transvaal, South Africa

Fat-tailed sheep, southwestern Cape, South Africa

Herd of antelope Battle Cave, Injasuti, Drakensberg, Natal

Ox, In Edjar, Tassili n'Ajjer, Algeria

Warthog, Giant's Castle, Drakensberg, Natal

Giraffe, Twyfelfontein, Namibia

Lion, Twyfelfontein, Namibia

Snake, Giant's Castle, Drakensberg, Natal

Hippopotamus,
Bothaville,
Orange Free State

Ostrich,
In Ejar, Tassili
n'Ajjer, Algeria

Baboon,
Giant's Castle,
Drakensberg,
Natal

Zebra,
Doornhoek,
Transvaal, South
Africa

Elephant and baby elephant,
Hex River
Mountains,
southwestern
Cape

GLOSSARY

adaptation: change or adjustment by which a species or individual improves its condition in relationship to its environment. Animals and plants may change in physical form or behaviour in order to live more efficiently in their habitat.

agriculture: the processes and activities associated with farming; the work of planting seeds, producing crops, and rearing animals.

archaeology: the scientific study of the life and culture of ancient peoples. Archaeology involves the excavation of ancient cities, relics, and artifacts.

artifact: any object made or crafted by human hands.

artisan: a skilled craftworker.

astronomy: the study of the stars and planets.

basin: all the land drained by a river and its tributaries. Water collects near a basin to form lakes.

biologists: scientists who study the life processes of plants and animals. Biologists chart growth and physical characteristics while also studying the environment.

caravan: a group of people travelling together through a desert. Camel caravans carried goods across the Sahara.

carcass: the body or remains of a dead animal.

ceramics: objects made of clay that are moulded into shape and baked in an oven.

continent: one of the principal land masses of the earth. Africa, Antarctica, Asia, Europe, North America, South America, and Australia are regarded as continents.

cult: a specific or distinct type of religious worship, including its own particular rules and ceremonies.

cultivate: to prepare land for the planting and growing of crops.

culture: the traditions, skills, habits, and systems of different groups of people at different times in history.

currency: the medium of exchange, or money used, in any country or region.

cursive: a style of writing in which the letters of each word are joined together, as opposed to printing.

deity: a god; a being who possesses a divine nature.

domestication: the process of taming wild animals and then using them for various purposes, such as food, a source of milk, or as beasts of burden.

dune: a hill of sand, frequently part of a desert landscape.

dynasty: a family of rulers; the period of time during which a specific family is in power.

environment: the circumstances or conditions of a plant or animal's surroundings. The physical and social conditions of an organism's environment influence its growth and development.

epoch: in history, a new and important period; a period of time considered in terms of important events, developments, or persons which dominate it. Also a geological division of time, of millions of years.

equator: an imaginary circle around the earth. The equator divides the earth's surface into the Northern Hemisphere and the Southern Hemisphere.

evolution: a gradual process in which a living thing such as an animal or plant changes into a different and usually more complex or better form. Groups of organisms may change with the passage of time so that descendants differ physically from their ancestors.

expedition: a journey or exploratory mission undertaken in order to achieve a specific purpose.

extinction: the process of destroying or extinguishing. Many species of plant and animal life face extinction because of natural changes in the environment or changes caused by the carelessness of humans.

fauna: the animals which live and thrive in a specific environment at a specific period in time. The fauna of any place on earth is determined by the ability to adapt to and grow in the existing environmental conditions.

flora: the plants which grow in a specific environment at a specific period of time. The earth's flora varies from place to place.

fossil: a hardened remnant or trace of an organism of a past geological age, such as a skeleton or leaf imprint, embedded in the rocks of the earth's crust. Scientists search for fossils as a way of learning about past life.

geography: the science which studies the earth's physical features, such as landscape, weather, and types of plants and animals.

geology: a branch of physical science that deals specifically with the earth and all its features.

glaciers: gigantic moving sheets of ice that covered great areas of the earth during the ice ages, and are now confined to near-polar and mountainous regions.

habitat: the areas or type of environment in which a person or other organism normally lives. Specific environmental factors are necessary for providing a "natural" habitat for all living things.

harpoon: a spear-like weapon with a barbed head used in hunting whales and large fish.

hemisphere: a half of the earth; the earth is divided in half by the equator into the Northern and Southern Hemispheres.

herbivore: an animal that eats plants.

hieroglyphic: a type of writing used by ancient Egyptians in which certain signs and symbols were used to represent words instead of letters.

hostile: having the qualities or characteristics of an enemy; unfriendly.

humid: containing a large amount of water or water vapour; damp. Warm air currents floating through coastal areas produce a humid climate.

lava: melted rock which flows from an erupting volcano.

marsh: an area of low-lying flat land, such as a swamp or bog. The marsh is a type of borderland between dry ground and water.

mercenary: hired soldier; soldier paid by a foreign country to fight in battle.

migrate: to move from place to place in search of food and shelter. Migration usually revolves around seasonal changes.

mollusc: any of a large group of animals having soft bodies enclosed in hard shells. Snails, oysters, and clams are molluscs.

monarch: the primary ruler of a state or kingdom, such as a king or queen.

monogamy: the practice of having only one partner or mate.

mummification: the technique of preserving the bodies of the dead, practised in Egypt and elsewhere.

nocturnal: of or having to do with the night; referring to animals that are active at night.

oligarchy: a government run by a few select people.

oracle: any person who is believed to be capable of speaking to or communicating with the gods.

pagan: a person who does not follow one of the world's major religions, but may hold traditional beliefs.

papyrus: a type of parchment or paper made from a plant which grew along the Nile River during the time of the ancient Egyptians.

perishable: likely to spoil.

pharaoh: a king or ruler of ancient Egypt.

plateau: an elevated and more or less level expanse of land.

polytheism: belief in the existence of more than one god, or many gods.

predator: an animal that lives by preying on others. Predators kill other animals for food.

prehensile: having limbs which are adapted for grasping or wrapping around something.

prey: an animal that is hunted and killed for food by another. Small animals are usually prey for larger ones.

rain forests: evergreen forests of the tropics, characterized by dense vegetation and heavy rainfall. Rain forests are very difficult to explore because of the thick vegetation.

rift: a split or chasm in the earth. The Great Rift Valley of Africa is 3,000 kilometres long.

ritual: a system of acts or procedures, especially concerned with religious worship.

sanctuary: a place of peace or safety; a haven or place of rest; a special building set aside for religious worship.

savanna: a treeless plain or grassland, characterized by scattered trees, especially in tropical or subtropical regions having seasonal rains.

schistosomiasis: a tropical disease of the vital organs caused by the invasion of parasites into blood vessels.

sovereign: a supreme ruler; one who possesses authority above all others.

species: a type of plant or animal.

stele: Greek for "pillar", an inscribed stone slab marking a grave or commemorating an event or person.

steppe: great plains with few trees and scrubby vegetation.

temperate: a climate which is neither very cold nor very hot, but moderate.

transhumance: the migratory movements and patterns of certain animals and the people who depend on them.

tributary: a small river or stream which usually flows into and is eventually part of a large one.

tuber: a plant whose fruit develops and grows underground. Potatoes are tubers.

valley: a stretch of low land that lies between hills or mountains and usually has a stream or river flowing through it.

vassal: a servant or slave.

INDEX

A

Abu Simbel, 57
Acheulian culture, 19, 24-25
Adulis, 54
Afar region, 12
Afar triangle, 10
Africa (province), 63
agriculture, 30, 48, 54
Akhenaton, 39
Aksum, 52-55
Alexander the Great, 58-60
Alexandria, 58, 60, 68
Algerian steppe, 30
Alodia, 51
Amenemhet, 36
Amenhotep IV, 39
Ammon, 59
Amon-Re, 59
anchorites, 69
Antonius, 69
Antony, Mark, 64
apes, 10-11
Archimedes, 60
art, prehistoric, 70-71
artifacts, stone 18-19
Assembly of the People, 45
Assyrian Empire, 56
Aterians, 21, 22
Aton, 38-39
Aton-Re, 38, 40
Australopithecus, 9, 12, 13
Australopithecus afarensis, 10
Australopithecus africanus, 12
Australopithecus robustus, 12, 13

B

Baal Hammon, 45
Bantu, 42
Battle of Actium, 64
Battle of Issus, 58
belts, 6
bifacial tools, 19, 21, 24
Black, Davidson, 9
blacksmiths, 42
Books of the Dead, 41
Broken Hill (Zambia), 16
Broom, Robert, 9
Bushmen, 25

C

cadastre, 33
calendar, 32
camel, 67
Carthage, 44-47, 62
cattle breeding, 48-49
cenobies, 69
ceramics, 26, 29
Channel of the Two Seas, 56-57
chips, 18-19, 21
Christianity, 68-69
Cleopatra, 64
clergy, 34-35
Congo Basin, 42
Congo River, 6
Coptic church, 68-69
Cosmas Indicopleustes, 52
cults, 65
culture, 18-19
Cyprian, 69

D

Darius III (king), 58
Dart, Raymond, 9
Darwin, Charles, 8
Dido, 44
Djenne, 42
Dubois, Eugène, 8-9
Dynasties, 32

E

Egypt, 32-65
    everyday life, 34
    intellectual class, 35
    Middle Kingdom, 36
    New Kingdom, 36
    priests, 34-35
    religion, 38-39, 40-41
    social structure, 35
Elephants, 49
Eratosthenes, 60
Ethiopic fauna, 20
Etruscans, 46
Euclid, 60
evolution, 8, 16, 17
extinction, 16

F

Fayum (oasis), 36
fire, 15
forest, equatorial, 22-23
fossils, 8-9, 16

G

glaciation periods, 21
goat-rearing, 26
gold, 33
Granicus River, 58
Great Rift, 6
Greece, 56-61

H

Hannibal, 46, 62
Heliopolis, 38, 40
Hellenistic monarchies, 60
herding, 30
Hermopolis, 38, 40
Herodotus, 57
hieratic writing, 32
hieroglyphic writing, 32
hominids, 10-11
Homo erectus, 13, 14-15, 16
Homo habilis, 12-13
Homo sapiens, 13, 16
humans (classification), 8
hunting, 19, 21
Hyksos, 36

I, J

iron, 51, 54
Iron Age, 42
irrigation, 48
Isis, 65
ivory, 54
Java, 9, 16
Johannesburg, 9
Johanson, Donald, 10

K

Kenyan Rift Valley, 14
Kingdom of the Delta, 32
Kingdom of the Valley, 32
Kush, 48-51

L

Laetoli (Tanzania), 10
Lake Chad, 20, 28
lakes, 6, 28-29
language, 14, 55
Large Council, 45
Lazaret (France), 15
Leakey, Louis, 9, 12
Leakey, Mary, 9, 10
Lepidus, Marcus, 64
Libya, 56
Linné, Carl von, 16
livestock-rearing, 54
"Lucy", 10, 12
Lupembians, 22-23

M

Makuria, 51
Masinissa (king), 62-63
Mauretania, 63
Mediterranean Sea, 14
Mediterranean ship, 46
Memphis, 32, 38, 40
Menes (king), 32
Meroe, 48, 50-51
microlith, 26
Middle Kingdom, 36, 40, 41
Middle Stone Age, 24
monasteries, 68
Mousterians, 21
mummification, 40

N

Napata, 48
Napier, John, 12
Neanderthal, 16
Neolithic period, 30, 32
New Kingdom, 36, 41
New Stone Age, 26
Niger River, 22, 42
Nile River, 6, 21, 26, 28, 30, 32, 34, 48
Nile Valley, 26, 32
Nobatia, 51
Nok society, 42
nomes, 32
Nubia, 51
Numidia, 63

O

Oasis of Siwa, 58-59
obelisks, 52
Octavian, 64
Old Kingdom, 32-33, 34
Olduvai (Tanzania), 13, 19
Omo (Ethiopia), 12
Oracle of Ammon, 59
Osiris, 41, 65

P

pebble tools, 18-19
Persian Empire, 58
pharaoh, 32
Philip II (king), 58
Phoenicia, 36
Phoenicians, 46
Pliocene epoch, 10-11
pottery, 29
pre-australopithecines, 10
primates, 8
Ptah, 38, 40
Ptolemies, 60, 65
Publius Petronius, 51
Punic civilization, 44-47
Punic Wars, 62-63
pyramids, 32-33, 36

R

rain forest, 6
religion, 16, 54-55, 65
rivers, 28-29
rock paintings, 16, 25, 31
Roman Empire, 65
Romans, 62, 63, 67
Rome, 62, 64-65, 66-67
Rosetta Stone, 33
Rufus, Curtius, 59

S

Sahara Desert, 6, 20-21, 30, 31, 42, 66, 67
Sahel, 22-23
Sangoans, 22-23
savanna, 6, 13, 19, 23, 25, 26
Scipio Africanus, 62
scrub zone, 6
Seleucids, 60
Septimius Severus, 68, 69
Serapis, 65
Small Council, 45
Stillbay-Pietersburg culture, 25
stone blades, 26
stone chipping, 24
stone tools, 18, 23
Strait of Messina, 62-63
Suez Canal, 57
suffets, 45
Syphax (king), 62

T

Takija Mariam, 52
Tanit, 45
Teilhard de Chardin, Pierre, 9
Temple of the Muses, 60
Tener region, 30, 31
Tertullian, 69
Texts of the Pyramids, 40
Thebes, 36
Thinite epoch, 32
Thoth, 38, 40
thrones, 52
Tibesti Mountains, 21
Tigris River, 56
Tobias, Philip, 12
tools, 19, 22, 23, 24, 26, 29, 34, 42
Transvaal, 9
travel, 42

V, W, Z

Valley of the Kings, 37
wheat, 64-65
writing, 55
Zama, 63
Zeus, 59
Zeus-Ammon, 59
Zinjanthropus boisei, 12
Zoser (king), 32-33